The REXX Language

The REXX Language
A Practical Approach to Programming

Second Edition

MICHAEL COWLISHAW
IBM UK Laboratories Ltd.

Prentice Hall, Englewood Cliffs, New Jersey 07632

Library of Congress Cataloging-in-Publication Data

Cowlishaw, M. F.
    The REXX language : a practical approach to programming / Mike
Cowlishaw. -- 2nd ed.
      p.   cm.
    ISBN 0-13-780651-5
    1. REXX (Computer program language)   I. Title.
QA76.73.R24C69 1990
005.13'3--dc20   89-71130
                                                                  CIP

Editorial/production supervision: **Karen Bernhaut**
Manufacturing buyer: **Kelly Behr**

 © 1990 by Prentice-Hall, Inc.
A Division of Simon & Schuster
Englewood Cliffs, New Jersey 07632

The publisher offers discounts on this book when ordered
in bulk quantities. For more information, write:

> Special Sales/College Marketing
> Prentice-Hall, Inc.
> College Technical and Reference Division
> Englewood Cliffs, New Jersey 07632

Printed in the United States of America

10 9 8 7 6 5 4 3

ISBN 0-13-780651-5

Prentice-Hall International (UK) Limited, *London*
Prentice-Hall of Australia Pty. Limited, *Sydney*
Prentice-Hall Canada Inc., *Toronto*
Prentice-Hall Hispanoamericana, S.A., *Mexico*
Prentice-Hall of India Private Limited, *New Delhi*
Prentice-Hall of Japan, Inc., *Tokyo*
Simon & Schuster Asia Pte. Ltd., *Singapore*
Editora Prentice-Hall do Brasil, Ltda., *Rio de Janeiro*

To Kittredge

Contents

Preface

The REXX programming language has been designed with just one objective. It has been designed to make programming easier than it was before, in the belief that the best way to foster high quality programs is to make writing them as simple and as enjoyable as possible. Each part of the language has been devised with this in mind; getting the design right for people to use is more important than providing for easy implementation.

Inevitably I have made compromises in ten years of working on REXX. Despite this, I believe that the language has achieved its objective and truly makes programming easier. I also believe (and hope) that future languages will improve on it – REXX is just a start in the direction of languages designed for people rather than for computers.

A programming language is a complex structure, typically characterized by its most visible aspect – its syntax. Of equal importance is its semantics, the meaning behind the instructions. But perhaps most important of all is the philosophy behind the language – the guiding principles that governed the decisions made as the language was designed.

The purpose of this book is to describe and define the REXX language, as of October 1989. I try to present the whole language; the syntax, the semantics, and the philosophy. It is intended that this will form a suitable reference for those planning for, using, or implementing REXX language processors. The background information will also provide a basis for discussions on the future of the language, and should help to answer the questions raised by students of the language.

This book is divided into two parts. The first, background, part includes a short introduction to REXX and a summary of its features, for those new to the language. This introduction is followed by descriptions of the concepts behind the language, the principles behind its design, and its history.

The second and major part is the language definition. This definition is mainly in prose, though a collection of syntax diagrams is provided as an appendix. The building blocks of the language are described first, followed by the control constructs and built-in functions. The final sections treat the semantics of the more complex areas in detail. There are numerous examples throughout, and also a "real" program which forms the second appendix.

There are two new appendices in this edition: one lists the changes since the first edition of this book, and the other is a glossary of the technical terms used in the book.

This second edition of the book does not include any major change of direction in the language. Rather, the additions are relatively small, but are powerful; they are made in ways consistent with the philosophy of the language and make it easier to write larger and more portable programs. There are also a number of minor improvements and clarifications.

Although this book is a complete and definitive description of the language, there is much more that can be said about REXX. For a general introduction to the language, and a description of some of its implementations, I recommend the companion volume to this work, *Modern Programming Using REXX*.[1]

Acknowledgments

The most important influence on the development of the REXX language was the IBM internal electronic network, VNET. Without the network (and the people who keep it running), there would have been little incentive to start a task of this magnitude; and without the constant flow of ideas and feedback from people using the network REXX would have been a much poorer language. Much credit for the effectiveness of VNET as a communication medium for this sort of work is due to Peter Capek who created the *VM Newsletter* (1977–1983). Today, REXX language design is carried out over the same network almost entirely with the aid of the TOOLS computer conference system[2] – appropriately enough, a system written in REXX.

Many languages and people have influenced the design of REXX, and it is difficult to say where many of the features originated. Perhaps the most significant is the language EXEC 2, by C. J. Stephenson. This, together

[1] R. P. O'Hara and D. R. Gomberg, **Modern Programming Using REXX**, *Prentice-Hall*, Second edition (1988) ISBN 0-13-579329-5.

[2] D. M. Chess and M. F. Cowlishaw, **A Large Scale Computer Conferencing System**, *IBM Systems Journal*, Volume 26, No. 1 (1987).

with an interface program known as the Yorktown SVC package (by Michel Hack), has strongly influenced the language; particularly in the area of generalized external interfaces. I am indebted to Michel Hack for numerous extensive discussions on the philosophies and features of both the REXX language and its interfaces.

One of the features of the language is its rich set of built-in functions. Their high quality is largely due to Steve Davies, who was responsible for their design and implementation for many years. Steve has made significant contributions throughout the language.

Members of the IBM Endicott Programming Laboratory (New York), especially Gary Brodock, Rick McGuire, Steve Price, and their colleagues, have also contributed much to REXX implementations. They have shown a rare sensitivity to the philosophy of the language; their implementations closely follow the concepts that originally led to the REXX language. I am happy to note that the same is true of all the REXX implementations I have seen – my thanks to those who have made this so. As REXX is implemented in increasingly diverse environments it seems that the fundamental philosophy and concepts remain valid.

A landmark in REXX history has been the development of a REXX compiler. This was based on research at IBM's Haifa Scientific Center in Israel and was then developed as a commercial product by the IBM Vienna Software Development Laboratory, in Austria. This new look at implementing REXX has led to numerous improvements in this book.

Over the years, hundreds of people have made constructive criticisms and comments on the REXX language and many have contributed code and documentation. Members of the informal REXX Language Committee, coordinated by Wes Christensen, were of special help in the decisions leading to major enhancements to the REXX language in the early 1980s.

All REXX users are indebted to those people from all over the world who have contributed help, suggestions, and time. I regret that I cannot give individual thanks to everybody, but I would like to mention those people who have contributed code or documentation to my original REXX implementation or to this book:

> Chuck Berghorn, Dave Betker, Reed Bittinger, Ian Brackenbury, Gary Brodock, Peter Capek, Steve Davies, Roderic Davis, Bertrand Denoix, Forrest Garnett, John Godwin, Rob Golden, Laurie Griffiths, Alfred Gschwend, Michel Hack, Rick Haeckel, Klaus Hansjakob, Gerry Hoernes, Ray Holland, Skip Knoble, Burn Lewis, Derek Lieber, Michael Lovelace, Ray Mansell, Brian Marks, Bob Marshall, Rick McGuire, Jim Mehl, Bert Moser, Simon Nash, Mike Nicholson, Walter Pachl, Steven Powell, Dick Snow, Nora Stevenson, Coyt Tillman, Carol Thompson, Jay Tunkel, Russ Williams.

This book has been edited entirely electronically, first using the STET (Structured Editing Tool) and XEDIT (System Product Editor) text editing programs, and later the LEXX Live Parsing Editor.[3] It was type-set using SCRIPT/VS, the Document Composition Facility. To Xavier de Lamberterie, Geoff Bartlett, Mike Kay, and to everyone else who has contributed to these tools, I offer my thanks. My thanks, too, to the experts at Prentice-Hall who have encouraged and advised me.

I must also thank IBM for permission to use the new material for the second edition of this book and for permission to use the material from my first paper describing REXX.[4]

Finally, I should like to thank Bob O'Hara for the original inspiration for this book, and for his considerable assistance with the formatting of both editions.

Mike Cowlishaw

---

[3] M. F. Cowlishaw, **LEXX – A programmable structured editor**, *IBM Journal of Research and Development*, Volume 31, No. 1 (1987).

[4] M. F. Cowlishaw, **The design of the REXX language**, *IBM Systems Journal*, Volume 23, No. 4 (1984).

The REXX Language

Part 1

Background

This introductory part of the book is in five sections. The first two sections introduce the REXX language, the next two sections describe the concepts and design principles that shaped it, and the final section reviews the history of the language.

SECTION 1: WHAT KIND OF A LANGUAGE IS REXX?

REXX is a procedural language that allows programs and algorithms to be written in a clear and structured way. The primary design goal has been that it should be genuinely easy to use both by computer professionals and by "casual" general users. A language that is designed to be easy to use must be effective at manipulating the kinds of symbolic objects that people normally deal with: words, numbers, names, and so on. Most of the features in REXX are included to make this kind of symbolic manipulation easy. REXX is also designed to be independent of its supporting system software, but with the capability of issuing both commands and conventional inter-language calls to its host environment.

The REXX language covers several application areas that traditionally have been served by fundamentally different types of programming language.

Personal programming

REXX is a language that provides powerful character and arithmetical abilities in a simple framework. You may write short programs with a minimum of overhead, yet facilities exist to allow the writing of robust large programs. The language is well adapted to interpretation, and is therefore rather suitable for many of the applications for which languages such as BASIC are currently used.

1

REXX has proved to be an easy language to learn and to teach. As a first language for students, it has the advantage of being a practical and structured programming language which is also easy to use and to debug.

Tailoring user commands

Command program interpreters are an important component of modern operating systems. Nearly all operating systems include some form of Executive, Shell, or Batch language. In many cases the language is so embedded into the operating system that it is unlikely to be of use outside its primary environment, but there is a clear trend towards providing command programming languages that are both powerful and capable of more general usage. REXX carries this principle further by being a language that is designed primarily for generality but also for suitability as a command programming language.

Over the years, many REXX programs for tailoring operating systems have been written – originally for the Conversational Monitor System component of the IBM Virtual Machine/System Product, and later for other operating systems. Many of these programs run to hundreds or thousands of lines, and some are in the tens of thousands. One laboratory that uses REXX has over four million lines of code written in REXX, with more than ten percent of the files on its main computer system being REXX programs.

Macros

Many applications are programmable by means of macros. In the data processing world there is a different macro language for almost every type of application. There are macro languages for editors, assemblers, interactive systems, text processors, spreadsheets, databases, and of course for other languages. The work of Stephenson[5] and others has highlighted the similarities between these applications, and the need for a common language. Since REXX is essentially a character manipulation language, it can provide the macro language for all these applications.

Macro languages often have unusual qualities and syntax that restrict their use to skilled programmers. REXX has a more conventional syntax and is a flexible language, and so makes it possible for the same jobs to be done in less time by less skilled personnel.

Prototype development

Interpreter implementations of REXX can be highly interactive, and permit rapid program development. This productivity advantage, together with the ease of interfacing REXX to system utilities for display

---

[5]   Stephenson, C. J. **On the structure and control of commands.** *ACM Operating Systems Review (SIGOPS)*, Vol 7, No 4, pp22-26 and 127-136 (1973).

and for data input and output, makes the language very suitable for modelling applications and products. It has also proved useful for setting up experimental systems for human factors studies.

The design of REXX is such that the same language can effectively and efficiently be used for many different applications that previously required the learning of several languages.

SECTION 2: SUMMARY OF THE REXX LANGUAGE

REXX is a language that is superficially similar to earlier languages. However, every aspect of the language has been critically reviewed and usually differs from other languages in ways that make REXX more suited to general users. It was possible to make these improvements because REXX was designed as an entirely new language, without the requirement that it be compatible with any earlier design.

The structure of a REXX program is extremely simple. This sample program, TOAST, is complete, documented, and executable as it stands.

TOAST

```
/* This wishes you the best of health. */
say 'Cheers!'
```

TOAST consists of two lines: the first is a comment that describes the purpose of the program, and the second is an instance of the SAY instruction. SAY simply displays the result of the expression following it – in this case a literal string.

Of course, REXX can do more than just display a character string. Although the language is composed of a small number of instructions and options, it is powerful. Where a function is not built-in it can be added by using one of the defined mechanisms for external interfaces.

The rest of this section introduces most of the features of REXX. It is intended as a brief introduction to the language to serve as a background for the rest of the book. Since many of the subtleties of REXX are best appreciated with use, you are urged to use the language yourself.

REXX provides a conventional selection of *control constructs*. These include IF... THEN... ELSE for simple conditional processing, SELECT... WHEN... OTHERWISE... END for selecting from a number of alternatives, and several varieties of DO... END for grouping and repetition. These constructs are similar to those of PL/I, but with several enhancements and simplifications. The DO (looping) construct can be used to step a variable TO some limit, FOR a specified number of iterations, and WHILE or UNTIL some condition is satisfied. DO FOREVER is also provided. Loop execution may be modified by LEAVE and ITERATE instructions that significantly reduce the complexity of many programs. No GOTO instruction is included, but a SIGNAL instruction is provided for abnormal transfer of control, such as error exits and computed branching.

REXX *expressions* are general, in that any operator combinations may be used (provided, of course, that the data values are valid for those operations). There are 9 arithmetic operators (including integer division, remainder, and power operators), 3 concatenation operators, 12 comparative operators, and 4 logical operators. All the operators act upon strings of characters, which may be of any length (typically limited only by the amount of storage available).

This sample program shows both expressions and a conditional instruction:

GREET

```
/* A short program to greet you.                        */
/* First display a prompt:                              */
say 'Please type your name and then press ENTER:'
parse pull answer          /* Get the reply into ANSWER */

/* If nothing was typed, then use a fixed greeting,     */
/* otherwise echo the name politely.                    */
if answer='' then say 'Hello Stranger!'
             else say 'Hello' answer'!'
```

The expression on the last SAY (display) instruction concatenates the string 'Hello' to the value of variable ANSWER with a blank in between them (the blank is here a valid operator, meaning "concatenate with blank"). The string '!' is then directly concatenated to the result built up so far. These simple and unobtrusive concatenation operators make it very easy to build up strings and commands, and may be freely mixed with the other operators.

The layout of control constructs is very flexible. In the GREET example, for instance, the IF construct could be laid out in a number of ways, according to personal preference. Line breaks can be added at either side of the THEN (or following the ELSE), or multiple instructions can be placed on one line with the aid of the semicolon separator.

In REXX, any string or symbol may be a *number*. Numbers are all "real" and may be specified in exponential notation if desired. (An implementation may use appropriately efficient internal representations, of course.) The arithmetic operations in REXX are designed for people rather for the machine, so are decimal rather than binary and have a number of user-oriented features. The operations are completely defined so that different implementations will always give the same results.

The NUMERIC instruction may be used to select the *arbitrary precision* of calculations (you may calculate with one thousand significant digits, for example). The same instruction may also be used to set the *fuzz* to be used for comparisons (that is, the number of significant digits of error permitted when making a numerical comparison) and the exponential notation (scientific or engineering) that REXX will use to present results.

Variables all hold strings of characters, and cannot have aliases under any circumstances. The simple *compound variable* mechanism allows the use of arrays (many-dimensional) that have the property of being indexed by arbitrary character strings. These are in effect content-addressable data structures, which can also be used for building lists and trees. Groups of variables (arrays) with a common stem to their name can be set, reset, or manipulated by references to that stem alone.

This example is a routine that removes all duplicate words from a string of words:

JUSTONE

```
/* This removes duplicate words from a string, and   */
/* shows the use of a compound variable (HADWORD)     */
/* which is indexed by arbitrary data (words).        */
Justone:  procedure      /* make all variables private */
   parse arg wordlist         /* get the list of words */
   hadword.=0         /* show all possible words as new */
   outlist=''              /* initialize the output list */
   do while wordlist¬=''    /* loop while we have data */
      /* split WORDLIST into first word and remainder    */
      parse var wordlist word wordlist
      if hadword.word then iterate  /* loop if had word */
      hadword.word=1  /* remember we have had this word */
      outlist=outlist word   /* add word to output list */
      end
   return outlist           /* finally return the result */
```

This example also shows some of the built-in *string parsing* available with the PARSE instruction. This provides a fast and simple way of decomposing strings of characters using a primitive form of pattern matching. A string may be split into parts using various forms of patterns, and then assigned to variables by words or as a whole.

A variety of internal and external calling mechanisms are defined. The most primitive is the *command* (which is quite similar to a *message* in the Smalltalk-80[6] system and in other object-oriented systems), in which a clause that consists of just an expression is evaluated. The resulting string of characters is passed to the currently selected external environment, which might be an operating system, an editor, or any other functional object. This ability to send commands to different environments is a primary concept of the language and is especially important when REXX is used as a "macro" language for extending applications.

---

[6]   See, for example: Xerox Learning Research Group, **The Smalltalk-80 system,** *Byte* **6**, No. 8, pp36-47 (August 1981).

The REXX programmer can also invoke *functions* and *subroutines*. These may be internal to the program, built-in (part of the language), or external. Within an internal routine, variables may be shared with the caller, or protected by the PROCEDURE instruction (that is, be made local to the routine). If protected, selected variables or groups of variables belonging to the caller may be exposed to the routine for read or write access.

Certain types of *exception handling* are supported. A simple mechanism (associated with the CALL and SIGNAL instructions) allows the trapping of run-time errors, halt conditions (external interrupts), command errors (errors resulting from external commands), stream (input and output) errors, and the use of uninitialized variables. Where appropriate it is possible to call a subroutine to handle the exception, and error handling is supported by a useful set of built-in functions.

The INTERPRET instruction (expected to be supported by interpreters only) allows any string of REXX instructions to be interpreted dynamically. It is useful for some kinds of interactive or interpretive environments, and can be used to build the following SHOWME program — an almost trivial "instant calculator":

SHOWME

```
/* Simple calculator that evaluates REXX expressions. */
numeric digits 20        /* Work to 20 digits              */
parse arg input          /* Get expression into INPUT */
interpret 'Say' input    /* Build and execute SAY         */
```

This program first sets REXX arithmetic to work to 20 digits. It then assigns the first argument string (perhaps typed by a user) to the variable INPUT. The final instruction evaluates the expression following the keyword INTERPRET to build a SAY instruction which is then executed. If you were to call this program with the argument "22/7" then the instruction "Say 22/7" would be built and executed. This would therefore display the result

```
3.1428571428571428571
```

Input and *output* functions in REXX are defined only for simple character-based operations. Included in the language are the concepts of named character streams (whose actual source or destination are determined externally). These streams may be accessed on a character basis or on a line-by-line basis. One input stream is linked with the concept of an *external data queue* that provides for limited formal communication with external programs.

A rich set of built-in functions is included. These provide extensive string and word manipulations, date and time extraction (in a variety of formats), conversions, bit manipulations, number manipulation and formatting, state and error handling, input and output, and random number generation.

The language defines an extensive *tracing* (debugging) mechanism, though it is recognized that some implementations may be unable to support the whole package or may prefer to provide an alternative process. The tracing options allow various subsets of instructions to be traced (Commands, Labels, All, and so on), and also control the tracing of various levels of expression evaluation results (intermediate calculation results, or just the final results). Furthermore, for a suitable implementation, the language describes an *interactive tracing* option, in which the execution of the program may be halted selectively. Once execution has paused, you may then type in any REXX instructions (to display or alter variables, and so on), step to the next pause, or re-execute the last clause traced.

An example, longer than those shown above, of a REXX program is included as the second appendix to this book, on page 171.

SECTION 3:   FUNDAMENTAL LANGUAGE CONCEPTS

Language design is always subtly affected by unconscious biases and by historical precedent. To minimize these effects a number of concepts were chosen and used as guidelines for the design of the REXX language. The following list includes the major concepts that were consciously followed during the design of REXX.

A complete treatment of some of these topics would fill another book, so unfortunately these paragraphs can only be summaries of the extensive discussions that led to the current design.

Readability

> If there is one concept that has dominated the evolution of REXX syntax, it is *readability* (used here in the sense of perceived legibility). Readability in this sense is a rather subjective quality, but the general principle followed in REXX is that the tokens which form a program can be written much as one might write them in Western European languages (English, French, and so forth). Although the semantics of REXX is, of course, more formal than that of a natural language, REXX is lexically similar to normal text.

> The structure of the syntax means that the language readily adapts itself to a variety of programming styles and layouts. This helps satisfy user preferences and allows a lexical familiarity that also increases readability. Good readability leads to enhanced understandability, thus yielding fewer errors both while writing a program and while reading it for information, debugging, or maintenance. Important factors here are:

> 1.   There is deliberate support throughout the language for upper and lower case letters, both for processing data and for the program itself.

2.   The essentially free format of the language (and the way blanks
      are treated around tokens and so on) lets you lay out the pro-
      gram in the style that you feel is the most readable.

3.   Punctuation is required only when absolutely necessary to
      remove ambiguity (though it may often be added according to
      personal preference, so long as it is syntactically correct). This
      relatively tolerant syntax has proved to be less frustrating than
      the syntax of languages such as Pascal.

4.   Modern concepts of structured programming are available in
      REXX, and can undoubtedly lead to programs that are easier to
      read than they might otherwise be. The structured program-
      ming constructs also make REXX a good language for teaching
      the concepts of good structure.

5.   Loose binding between lines and program source ensure that
      even though programs are affected by line ends, they are not
      irrevocably so. You may spread a clause over several lines or
      put it on just one line. Clause separators are optional (except
      where more than one clause is put on a line), again letting you
      adjust the language to your own preferred style.

Natural data typing

"Strong typing", in which the values that a variable may take are
tightly constrained, first became a fashionable attribute for languages
in the 1970s. I believe that the greatest advantage of strong typing
is for the interfaces between program modules, where errors may be
difficult to catch. Errors *within* modules that would be detected by
strong typing (and would not be detected from context) are much
rarer, certainly when compared with design errors, and in the
majority of cases do not justify the added program complexity.

REXX, therefore, treats types as naturally as possible. The meaning
of data depends entirely on their usage. All values are defined in the
form of the symbolic notation (strings of characters) that a user would
normally write to represent that data. Since no internal or machine
representation is exposed in the language, the need for many data
types is reduced. There are, for example, no fundamentally different
concepts of *integer* and *real*; there is just the single concept of
number. The results of all operations have a defined symbolic representation, so you can always inspect values (for example, the intermediate results of an expression evaluation). Numeric computations
and all other operations are precisely defined, and will therefore act
consistently and predictably for every correct implementation.

This language definition does not exclude the future addition of a data
typing mechanism for those applications that require it, though there
seems to be little call for this. The mechanism could perhaps be in
the form of ASSERT-like instructions that assign data type checking

to variables during execution flow. An optional restriction, similar to the existing trap for uninitialized variables, could be defined to provide enforced assertion for all variables.

Emphasis on symbolic manipulation

The values that REXX manipulates are (from the user's point of view, at least) in the form of strings of characters. It is extremely desirable to be able to manage this data as naturally as you would manipulate words on a page or in a text editor. The language therefore has a rich set of character manipulation operators and functions.

Concatenation, the most common string operation, is treated specially in REXX. In addition to a conventional concatenate operator ("||"), there is a novel *blank operator* that concatenates two data strings together with a blank in between. Furthermore, if two syntactically distinct terms (such as a string and a variable name) are abutted, then the data strings are concatenated directly. These operators make it especially easy to build up complex character strings, and may at any time be combined with the other operators available.

For example, the SAY instruction consists of the keyword SAY followed by any expression. In this instance of the instruction, if the variable N has the value '6' then

```
say n*100/50'%' ARE REJECTS
```

would display the string

```
12% ARE REJECTS
```

Concatenation has a lower priority than the arithmetic operators. The order of evaluation of the expression is therefore first the multiplication, then the division, then the direct concatenation, and finally the two "concatenate with blank" operations.

Since the concatenation operators are distinct from the arithmetic operators, very natural coercion (automatic conversion) between numbers and character strings is possible and has become a highly valued feature of the language.

Dynamic scoping

Most languages (especially those designed to be compiled) rely on static scoping, where the physical position of an instruction in the program source may alter its meaning. Languages that are interpreted (or that have advanced compilers) generally have *dynamic scoping*. Here, the meaning of an instruction is only affected by the instructions that have already been executed (rather than those that precede or follow it in the program source).

REXX scoping is purely dynamic. This implies that it may be efficiently interpreted because only minimal look-ahead is needed. It also implies that a compiler is harder to implement, so the semantics includes restrictions that ease the task of the compiler writer. Most importantly, though, it implies that in general a person reading the program need only be aware of the program *above* the point which is being studied. Not only does this aid comprehension, but it also makes programming and maintenance easier when only a computer display terminal is being used.

The GOTO instruction is a necessary casualty of dynamic scoping. In a truly dynamically scoped language, a GOTO cannot be used as an error exit from a loop. If it were, the loop would never become inactive.[7] REXX instead provides an "abnormal transfer of control" instruction, SIGNAL, that terminates all active control structures when it is executed. Note that it is not just a synonym for GOTO since it cannot be used to transfer control within a loop (for which alternative instructions are provided).

Nothing to declare

Consistent with the philosophy of simplicity, REXX provides no mechanism for declaring variables. Variables may of course be documented and initialized at the start of a program, and this covers the primary advantages of declarations. The other, data typing, is discussed above.

Implicit declarations do take place during execution, but the only true declarations in the REXX language are the markers (*labels*) that identify points in the program that may be used as the targets of SIGNAL instructions or internal routine calls.

System independence

The REXX language is independent of both system and hardware. REXX programs, though, must be able to interact with their environment. Such interactions necessarily have system dependent attributes. However, these system dependencies are clearly bounded and the rest of the language has no such dependencies. In some cases this leads to added expense in implementation (and in language usage), but the advantages are obvious and well worth the penalties.

As an example, string-of-characters comparison is normally independent of leading and trailing blanks. (The string " Yes " *means* the same as "Yes" in most applications.) However, the influence of underlying hardware has subtly affected this kind of decision, so that many languages only allow trailing blanks but not leading blanks. By contrast, REXX permits both leading and trailing blanks during general comparisons.

---

[7] Some interpreted languages detect control jumping outside the body of the loop and terminate the loop if this occurs. These languages are therefore relying on static scoping.

Limited span syntactic units

The fundamental unit of syntax in the REXX language is the clause, which is a piece of program text terminated by a semicolon (usually implied by the end of a line). The span of syntactic units is therefore small, usually one line or less. This means that the syntax parser in the language processor can rapidly detect and locate errors, which in turn means that error messages can be both precise and concise.

It is difficult to provide good diagnostics for languages (such as Pascal and its derivatives) that have large fundamental syntactic units. For these languages, a small error can often have a major or distributed effect on the parser, which can lead to multiple error messages or even misleading error messages.

Dealing with reality

A computer language is a tool for use by real people to do real work. Any tool must, above all, be reliable. In the case of a language this means that it should do what the user expects. User expectations are generally based on prior experience, including the use of various programming and natural languages, and on the human ability to abstract and generalize.

It is difficult to define exactly how to meet user expectations, but it helps to ask the question "Could there be a high *astonishment factor* associated with this feature?". If a feature, accidentally misused, gives apparently unpredictable results, then it has a high astonishment factor and is therefore undesirable.

Another important attribute of a reliable software tool is *consistency*. A consistent language is by definition predictable and is often elegant. The danger here is to assume that because a rule is consistent and easily described, it is therefore simple to understand. Unfortunately, some of the most elegant rules can lead to effects that are completely alien to the intuition and expectations of a user who, after all, is human.

Consistency applied for its own sake can easily lead to rules that are either too restrictive or too powerful for general human use. During the design process, I found that simple rules for REXX syntax quite often had to be rethought to make the language a more usable tool.

REXX originally allowed almost all options on instructions to be variable (and even the names of functions were variable), but many users fell into the pitfalls that were the side-effects of this powerful generality. For example, the TRACE instruction allows its options to be abbreviated to a single letter (as it needs to be typed often during debugging sessions). Users therefore often used the instruction "TRACE I", but when **I** had been used as a variable (perhaps as a loop counter) then this instruction could become "TRACE 10" – a correct but unexpected action. The TRACE instruction was therefore changed to treat the symbol as a constant (and the language became more complex as a consequence) to protect users against such happenings; a VALUE option on TRACE allows variability for the experienced user. There is a fine line to tread between concise (terse) syntax and usability.

Be adaptable

Wherever possible the language allows for extension of instructions and other language constructs. For example, there is a useful set of common characters available for future extensions, since only a restricted set is allowed for the names of variables (symbols). Similarly, the rules for keyword recognition allow instructions to be added whenever required without compromising the integrity of existing programs that are written in the appropriate style. There are no globally reserved words (though a few are reserved within the local context of a single clause).

A language needs to be adaptable because *it certainly will be used for applications not foreseen by the designer*. Although proven effective as a command programming and personal language, REXX may (indeed, probably will) prove inadequate in certain future applications. Room for expansion and change is included to make the language more adaptable.

Keep the language small

Every suggested addition to the language has been considered only if it would be of use to a significant number of users. The intention has been to keep the language as small as possible, so that users can rapidly grasp most of the language. This means that:

- The language appears less formidable to the new user.

- Documentation is smaller and simpler.

- The experienced user can be aware of all the abilities of the language, and so has the whole tool at his or her disposal to achieve results.

- There are few exceptions, special cases, or rarely used embellishments.

- The language is easier to implement.

No defined size or shape limits

The language does not define limits on the size or shape of any of its tokens or data (although there may be implementation restrictions). It does, however, define the *minimum* requirements that must be satisfied by an implementation. Wherever an implementation restriction has to be applied, it is recommended that it should be of such a magnitude that few (if any) users will be affected.

Where implementation limits are necessary, the language encourages the implementer to use familiar and memorable values for the limits. For example 250 is preferred to 255, 500 to 512, and so on. There is no longer any excuse for forcing the artifacts of the binary system onto a population that uses only the decimal system. Only a tiny minority of future programmers will need to deal with base-two-derived number systems.

SECTION 4:   DESIGN PRINCIPLES

A good philosophy for a language is of little use if there is not an effective process for testing the resulting design and tuning it to the needs of its users. As REXX evolved, so too did a certain design ethic; these principles are still followed today for REXX – other projects, too, are using similar techniques.

The design process started rather conventionally – the language was first designed and documented; this initial informal specification was then circulated to a number of appropriate reviewers. The revised initial description then became the basis for the first specification and implementation.

From then on, other less common design principles were followed. The most significant was the intense use of a communications network, but all three items in this list have had a considerable influence on the evolution of REXX.

Communications

Once an initial implementation was complete, the most important factor in the development of REXX began to take effect. IBM has an internal network, known as VNET, that at the time linked nearly 1000 mainframe computers in 40 countries. REXX rapidly spread throughout this network, so from the start many hundreds of people were using the language. All the users, from temporary staff to professional programmers, were able to provide immediate feedback to the designer on their preferences, needs, and suggestions for changes. (At times it seemed as though most of them did – at peak periods I was replying to an average of 350 pieces of electronic mail each day.)

An informal language committee soon appeared spontaneously, communicating entirely electronically, and the language discussions grew to be hundreds of thousands of lines.

On occasions it became clear as time passed that incompatible changes to the language were needed. Here the network was both a hindrance and a help. It was a hindrance as its size meant that REXX was enjoying very wide usage and hence many people had a heavy investment in existing programs. It was a help because it was possible to communicate directly with the users to explain why the change was necessary, and to provide aids to help and persuade people to change to the new version of the language. The decision to make an incompatible change was never taken lightly, but because changes could be made relatively easily the language was able to evolve much further than would have been the case if only upwards compatible extensions were considered.

Documentation before implementation

Every major section of the REXX language was documented (and circulated for review) before implementation. The documentation was not in the form of a functional specification, but was instead complete reference documentation that in due course became part of this language definition. At the same time (before implementation) sample programs were written to explore the usability of any proposed new feature. This approach resulted in the following benefits:

- The majority of usability problems were discovered before they became embedded in the language and before any implementation included them.

- Writing the documentation was found to be the most effective way of spotting inconsistencies, ambiguities, or incompleteness in a design. (But the documentation must itself be complete, to "final draft" standard.)

- I deliberately did not consider the implementation details until the documentation was complete. This minimized the implementation's influence upon the language.

- Reference documentation written after implementation is likely to be inaccurate or incomplete, since at that stage the author will know the implementation too well to write an objective description.

The language user is usually right

User feedback was fundamental to the process of evolution of the REXX language. Although users can occasionally be naïve in their suggestions, even those suggestions which appeared to be shallow were considered carefully since they often acted as pointers to deficiencies in the language or documentation. The language has often been tuned to meet user expectations; some of the desirable quirks of the language are a direct result of this necessary tuning. Much would have remained unimproved if users had had to go though a formal suggestions procedure instead of simply sending a piece of electronic mail directly to me. All of this mail was reviewed some time after the initial correspondence in an effort to perceive trends and generalities that might not have been apparent on a day-to-day basis.

Many (if not most) of the good ideas embodied in the language came directly or indirectly from suggestions made by users. It is impossible to overestimate the value of the direct feedback from users that was available while REXX was being designed.

SECTION 5: HISTORY

The REXX language (originally called "REX") borrows from many earlier languages; PL/I, Algol, and even APL have had their influences, as have several unpublished languages that I developed during the 1970's.

The language has developed in two distinct phases: the first being the rapid evolution of the language in an essentially experimental environment, and the second being a more cautious series of enhancements following the commercial availability of implementations of the language.

The first phase took place as a personal project of about four thousand hours during the years 1979 through 1982, at the IBM UK Laboratories near Winchester (England) and at the IBM T. J. Watson Research Center in New York (USA). With this background REXX has an international flavour, with roots in both the European and North American programming cultures.

In 1983, my own System/370 implementation became part of the Virtual Machine/System Product, as the System Product Interpreter for the Conversational Monitor System (CMS). This implementation of the language is described in the Reference Manual for that product.[8] In 1985 the first edition of this book was published, and soon after that the pioneer non-IBM implementation of REXX was announced by the Mansfield Software Group: this implementation runs under the MS-DOS and PC-DOS operating systems for Personal Computers. A number of other implementations have followed from a variety of suppliers: one which perhaps best demonstrates the suitability of REXX for different environments is a version for the Commodore Amiga computer.

The next milestone for REXX was its choice by IBM as the Procedures Language for the Systems Application Architecture (SAA).[9] This 1987 announcement implies a common REXX language across all the SAA operating systems: VM, MVS, OS/400, and OS/2.[10] The language interpreter development for all these environments is coordinated at the IBM Endicott Programming Laboratory, New York.

All the first implementations of REXX were interpreters: notable, then, was the announcement in 1989 of IBM's CMS REXX Compiler, developed at the IBM Vienna Software Development Laboratory in Austria with help from the IBM Scientific Centre at Haifa in Israel.

---

[8] **IBM Virtual Machine/System Product: System Product Interpreter Reference.** *IBM Reference Manual*, Order No. SC24-5239, IBM (1983).

[9] The Procedures Language for SAA comprises the REXX language, Double Byte Character Set support, and a series of common interfaces to the language.

[10] More formally: CMS in the VM/System Product or VM/Extended Architecture, TSO/E in the Enterprise Systems Architecture/370, Operating System/400 for the Application System/400 (AS/400), and Operating System/2 Extended Edition.

Inevitably the commercial exploitation of the language has required a stable language definition – the radical changes in the language that were characteristic of its first years are no longer possible. Fortunately, those early years of heavy use and rapid evolution probably mean that such radical changes are no longer necessary: rather one would expect to see incremental changes and adjustments consistent with the philosophy of keeping the language small and approachable. Even so it is not impossible that major enhancements could be added to the base REXX language: over the years there have been research proposals for both a REXX "systems programming language" and an object-oriented REXX. REXX will doubtless continue to evolve as software technology itself evolves. I hope, and expect, that even as it changes it will always remain true to its original goal.

Part 2

REXX Language Definition

This part of the book describes the REXX language, version 4.00. Changes to the language since the first edition of this book (version 3.60) are described in the appendix on page 175.

The language is described first in terms of the characters from which it is composed and its low-level syntax, and then progressively through more complex constructions. Finally, special sections describe the semantics of the more complicated areas.

SECTION 1: CHARACTERS AND ENCODINGS

Characters have meaning for REXX in two ways:

1.   A REXX program is itself built from characters.

2.   A REXX program manipulates data which are also characters.

In the definition of a programming language it is important to emphasise the distinction between a *character* and the *coded representation*[11] (encoding) of a character. The character "A", for example, is the first letter of the English alphabet, and this meaning is independent of any specific coded representation of that character. Different coded character sets (such as, for example, ASCII and EBCDIC)[12] use quite different encodings for this character (decimal values 65 and 193, respectively).

---

[11] These terms have the meanings as defined by the International Organization for Standardization, in ISO 2382 *Data processing – Vocabulary*.

[12] American Standard Code for Information Interchange, and Extended Binary Coded Decimal Interchange Code.

Except where stated otherwise, this book uses characters to convey meaning and not to imply a specific character code (the exceptions are certain built-in functions that specifically convert between characters and their represent-ations). At no time is REXX concerned with the glyph (actual appearance) of a character.

Character Sets

Programming in the REXX language can be considered to involve the use of two character sets. The first is used for expressing the REXX program itself, and is the relatively small set of characters described in the next section. The second character set is the set of characters that can be used as data by a particular implementation of a REXX language processor. This character set may be limited in size (often to a limit of 256 different characters, which have a convenient 8-bit representation), or it may be much larger. Usually, most or all of these characters are also allowed within a REXX program, but only within commentary or immediate (literal) data.

The REXX language explicitly defines the first character set, in order that programs will be portable and understandable; at the same time it avoids restrictions due to the language itself on the character set used for data. However, where the language itself manipulates or inspects the data (as when carrying out arithmetic operations), there may be requirements on the data character set (for example, numbers can only be expressed if there are digit characters in the set).

SECTION 2:   STRUCTURE AND GENERAL SYNTAX

A REXX program is built up out of a series of *clauses* that are composed of: zero or more blanks (which are ignored); a sequence of tokens (described in this section); zero or more blanks (again ignored); and the delimiter ";" (semicolon) which may be implied by line-end, certain keywords, or the colon ":" (if it follows a single symbol). Conceptually, each clause is scanned from left to right before execution and the tokens composing it are identified. Instruction keywords are recognized at this stage, comments (described below) are removed, and multiple blanks (except within literal strings) are reduced to single blanks. Blanks adjacent to operator characters and special characters (see below on page 22) are also removed.

Comments

Commentary is included in a REXX program by means of *comments*. A com-ment is started by the sequence of characters "/*", and is ended by "*/". Within these delimiters any characters are allowed. Comments may be nested, which is to say that "/*" and "*/" must pair correctly. Comments may be anywhere, and may be of any length. They have no effect on the program, except that they do act as separators (*i.e.*, two tokens with just a comment in between are not treated as a single token).

Example:

```
/* This is a valid comment */
```

Note: It is recommended that REXX programs start with a comment describing the program. Not only is this good programming practice, but some implementations may use this to distinguish REXX programs from other languages.

Implementation minimum: Implementations should support nested comments to a depth of at least 10. The length of a comment should not be restricted, in that it should be possible to "comment out" an entire program.

Tokens

The essential components of clauses are called *tokens*. These may be of any length, unless limited by implementation restrictions,[13] and are separated by blanks or by the nature of the tokens themselves.

The tokens are:

Literal strings

A sequence including **any** characters and delimited by the single quote character (') or the double-quote ("). Use "" to include a " in a literal string delimited by ", and similarly use two single quotes to include a single quote in a literal string delimited by single quotes. A literal string is a constant and its contents will never be modified by REXX. Literal strings must be complete on a single line (this means that unmatched quotes may be detected on the line that they occur).

Any string with no characters (*i.e.*, a string of length 0) is called a *null string*.

Examples:

```
'Fred'
"Don't Panic!"
'You shouldn''t'     /* Same as "You shouldn't" */
''                   /* A null string */
```

Implementation minimum: Implementations should support literal strings of at least 100 characters. (But note that the length of expression results, *etc.*, should have a much larger minimum, normally only limited by the amount of storage available.)

Note: Literal strings may also be defined in hexadecimal or in binary, if required. Anywhere that a literal string is allowed it may be followed

---

[13] Where implementation restrictions are applied, the size of the restriction should be a number that is readily memorable in the decimal system. 500 is preferred to 512, the number 250 is more natural than 256, and so on.

immediately by an "X" symbol (in which case it is taken to be a hexade-
cimal-defined literal string) or by a "B" symbol (in which case it is a
binary-defined literal string). These forms are now described in detail.

Hexadecimal Strings

Any sequence of zero or more hexadecimal digits (0-9, a-f, A-F), grouped
in pairs. The first group may have an odd number of digits, in which
case a '0' digit is assumed to the left of the first digit. The groups of
digits are optionally separated by one or more blanks, and the whole
sequence is delimited by single quotes or double-quotes and immediately
followed by the character "x" or "X". (The X may not be part of a longer
token.) The blanks, which may only be present at byte boundaries (and
may not be present at the beginning or end of the string), are to aid
readability and are ignored.

A hexadecimal string is a literal string formed by packing the hexadecimal codes given. It allows characters to be included in a program even
if the characters themselves cannot be entered directly.

Examples:

```
'ABCD'x
"1d ec f8"X
'123 45'x    /* Same as '01 23 45'x */
''x          /* Same as '' */
```

Implementation minimum: Implementations should support hexadecimal strings whose packed length is at least 100 characters.

Binary Strings

Any sequence of zero or more binary digits (0 or 1), grouped in fours.
The first group may have fewer than four digits, in which case up to
three '0' digits are assumed to the left of the first digit, to make a total
of four digits. The groups of digits are optionally separated by one or
more blanks, and the whole sequence is delimited by single quotes or
double-quotes and immediately followed by the character "b" or "B".
(The B may not be part of a longer token.) The blanks, which may only
be present between the groups of digits (and may not be present at the
beginning or end of the string), are to aid readability and are ignored.

A binary string is a literal string formed by packing the binary codes
given. If there are an odd number of groups of binary digits, four '0'
digits are added on the left before the digits are packed. Binary strings
allow characters to be specified explicitly, bit-by-bit.

Examples:

```
'11110000'b         /* == 'f0'x */
"101 1101"b         /* == '5d'x */
'1'b                /* == '00000001'b and '01'x */
'10000 10101010'b   /* == '0001 0000 1010 1010'b */
''b                 /* == '' */
```

Implementation minimum: Implementations should support binary strings whose packed length is at least 50 characters.

Symbols

Symbols are groups of any characters, selected from the English alphabetic and numeric characters (A-Z, a-z, 0-9) and/or from the characters . ! ? and underscore.[14] Any lower case alphabetic character in a symbol is translated to upper case before use.

Examples:

```
fred
Dan.Yr.Ogof
HI!
```

A symbol may include other characters in one situation only. If a symbol starts with a digit (0-9) or period it may end with the sequence "E" (or "e"), followed immediately by an optional sign ("+" or "-"), followed immediately by one or more digits (which may not be followed by any other symbol characters).[15] The symbol thus defined may be a number in exponential notation, for example:

```
17.3E-12
.03E+9
```

The meaning of a symbol depends on the context in which it is used. A symbol may be a constant (such as a number), a keyword, or the name of a variable. For details, see pages 32-37.

Implementation minimum: Implementations should support symbols of at least 50 characters. (But note that the length of its value, if it is a variable, should have a much larger limit.)

---

[14] Implementations may also informally allow characters such as national currency symbols (including the symbols for dollar, cent, and pound-sterling), accented and other language-specific characters, or the characters @ or #. Use of these characters is best avoided, however, as programs written using them are often not portable between different countries and between different computer systems.

[15] The sign in this context is part of the symbol; it is not an operator.

Operator characters

The characters + - * / % | & = ¬ \ > < are used (sometimes in combination) to indicate operations in expressions (see pages 25-27). A few of these are also used in parsing templates, and the equal sign is also used to indicate assignment. Blanks adjacent to operator characters are removed, so, for example, the sequences:

```
345>=123
345 >=123
345 >=   123
345 > =   123
```

are identical in meaning.

Some of these characters may not be available in all character sets, and if this is the case appropriate translations may be used.

Note that throughout the language, the *not* symbol, "¬", is synonymous with the backslash ("\"). The two symbols may be used interchangeably according to availability and personal preference.

Special characters

The characters , ; :) (together with the operator characters have special significance when found outside of literal strings, and constitute the set of "special" characters. They all act as token delimiters, and blanks adjacent to any of these are removed, with the exception that a blank adjacent to the outside of a parenthesis is only deleted if it is also adjacent to another special character (unless this is a parenthesis and the blank is outside it, too).

To illustrate how a clause is composed out of tokens, consider this example:

```
'REPEAT'   B + 3;
```

This is composed of six tokens: a literal string, a blank operator (described later), a symbol (which may have a value), an operator, a second symbol (a number), and a semicolon. The blanks between the "B" and the "+" and between the "+" and the "3" are removed. However one of the blanks between the "REPEAT" and the "B" remains as an operator. Thus the clause is treated as though written:

```
'REPEAT' B+3;
```

Implied semicolons and continuations

REXX will normally assume (imply) a semicolon at the end of each line, except if:

1. The line ends in the middle of a comment.

2. The last token was a comma. In this case the comma is functionally replaced by a blank, and hence acts as a *continuation character*.[16]

This means that semicolons need only be included to separate multiple clauses on a single line.

Notes:

1. Semicolons are added automatically by REXX after colons (when following a single symbol, a label) and after certain keywords when in the correct context. The keywords that may have this effect are ELSE, OTHERWISE, and THEN. These special cases reduce program entry errors significantly.

2. The two characters forming the comment delimiters "/ *" and "* /" must not be split by a line-end since they could not then be recognized correctly: an implied semicolon would be added.

---

[16] Note that a comment is not a token, so therefore a comment may follow the continuation character on a line.

SECTION 3:   EXPRESSIONS AND OPERATORS

Many clauses can include *expressions*. Expressions in REXX are a general mechanism for combining one or more pieces of data in various ways to produce a result, usually different from the original data.

Expressions consist of one or more *terms* (literal strings, symbols, function calls, or sub-expressions), and zero or more *operators* that denote operations to be carried out on terms. Most operators act on two terms, and there will be at least one of these *dyadic* operators between every pair of terms.[17] There are also *prefix* (monadic) operators, that act on the term that is immediately to the right of the operator. There may be one or more prefix operators to the left of any term.

Terms may be

- *Literal strings* (character strings delimited by quotes), which are constants.

- *Symbols* (no quotes), which are translated to upper case. Those that do not begin with a digit or a period may be the name of a variable, in which case the value of that variable is used. Otherwise they are treated as a constant string. A symbol may also be *compound*. See page 32.

- *Function calls*, which are of the form

    symbol([*expression*] [, [*expression*]] ...)

  or

    string([*expression*] [, [*expression*]] ...)

  See page 77.

- *Sub-expressions*, which consist of any expression bracketed by a left and a right parenthesis.

Evaluation of an expression is left to right, modified by parentheses and by operator precedence in the usual "algebraic" manner (see page 28). Expressions are wholly evaluated, except when an error occurs during evaluation.

As each term is used in an expression, it is evaluated as appropriate. The result is a "typeless" character string.[18] Consequently, the result of evaluating any expression is itself a typeless character string. All terms and results may be the *null string* (a character string of length 0). Note that the REXX language

---

[17] One operator, direct concatenation, is implied if two terms abut.

[18] These strings are described as typeless because they are not (as in many other programming languages) of a particular, declared type, such as binary, hexadecimal, integer, or array.

imposes no restriction on the maximum length of results, but there will usually be some practical limitation dependent upon the amount of storage and other resources available during execution.

The operators are constructed from one or more operator characters (see page 22). Blanks (and comments) adjacent to operator characters have no effect on the operator, and so the operators constructed from more than one character may have embedded blanks and comments. In addition, one or more blank characters, where they occur within expressions but are not adjacent to another operator, also act as an operator.

The operators may be subdivided into four groups: concatenation, arithmetic, comparative, and logical operators.

Concatenation

The concatenation operators are used to combine two strings to form one string by appending the second string to the right-hand end of the first string. The concatenation may occur with or without an intervening blank:

(blank)   Concatenate terms with one blank in between.

|| Concatenate without an intervening blank.

(abuttal)   Concatenate without an intervening blank.

Concatenation without a blank may be forced by using the || operator, but it is useful to remember that when two terms are adjacent and are not separated by an operator,[19] they will be concatenated in the same way. This is the *abuttal* operation. For example, if the variable TOTAL had the value '37.4', then Total'%' would evaluate to '37.4%'.

Arithmetic

Character strings that are numbers (see page 27) may be combined using the arithmetic operators:

+   Add.

-            Subtract.

*   Multiply.

/   Divide.

%   Integer divide.
             Divide and return the integer part of the result.

//   Remainder.
             Divide and return the remainder (not modulo, as the result may be negative).

---

[19] This can occur when the terms are syntactically distinct (such as a literal string and a symbol), or when they are separated only by a comment.

**   Power.
                Raise a number to a whole number power.

`Prefix` -   Same as the subtraction: "0 - number".

`Prefix` +   Same as the addition: "0+number".

See the section on **Numbers and Arithmetic** (page 127) for details of numeric precision, the format of valid numbers, and the operation rules for arithmetic. Note that if an arithmetic result is shown in exponential notation, then it is likely that rounding has occurred.

Comparative

The comparative operators compare two terms and return the value '1' if the result of the comparison is true, or '0' otherwise. Two sets of operators are defined: the *strict* comparisons and the *normal* comparisons.

The strict comparative operators all have one of the characters defining the operator doubled. The "==", "¬==", and "\==" operators test for strict equality or inequality between two strings. Two strings must be identical to be considered strictly equal. Similarly, the other strict comparative operators (such as ">>" or "<<") carry out a simple character-by-character comparison, with no padding of either of the strings being compared. If one string is shorter than, and is a leading sub-string of, another then it is smaller (less than) the other.

For all the other comparative operators, if **both** the terms involved are numeric,[20] a numeric comparison (in which leading zeros are ignored, *etc.* – see page 134) is effected; otherwise, both terms are treated as character strings. For this character string comparison, leading and trailing blanks are ignored, and then the shorter string is padded with blanks on the right. The character comparison operation is case sensitive, and (as for strict comparisons) the exact collating order may depend on the character set used for the implementation.[21]

The comparative operators return true ('1') if the terms are:

Normal comparative operators:

=   Equal (numerically or when padded, *etc.*).

¬= , \=   Not equal (inverse of =).

>   Greater than.

<   Less than.

---

[20] That is, if they can be compared numerically without error.

[21] For example, in an ASCII environment, the digits 0-9 are lower than the alphabetics, and lower case alphabetics are higher than upper case alphabetics. In an EBCDIC environment, lower case alphabetics precede upper case, but the digits are higher than all the alphabetics.

><, <>	Greater than or less than (same as "Not equal").
>=, ¬<, \<	Greater than or equal to, not less than.
<=, ¬>, \>	Less than or equal to, not greater than.

Strict comparative operators:

==	Strictly equal (identical).
¬==, \==	Strictly not equal (inverse of ==).
>>	Strictly greater than.
<<	Strictly less than.
>>=, ¬<<, \<<	Strictly greater than or equal to, strictly not less than.
<<=, ¬>>, \>>	Strictly less than or equal to, strictly not greater than.

Logical (Boolean)

A character string is taken to have the value "false" if it is '0', and "true" if it is '1'. The logical operators take one or two such values (values other than '0' or '1' are not allowed) and return '0' or '1' as appropriate:

&	And. Returns 1 if both terms are true.
|	Inclusive or. Returns 1 if either term is true.
&&	Exclusive or. Returns 1 if either (but not both) is true.
Prefix ¬, \	Logical not. Negates; 1 becomes 0 and *vice versa*.

Numbers

The arithmetic operators above require that both terms involved be numbers; similarly some of the comparative operators carry out a numeric comparison if both terms are numbers.

Numbers are introduced and defined in detail on pages 127-138. In summary, *numbers* are character strings consisting of one or more decimal digits optionally prefixed by a plus or minus sign, and optionally including a single period (".") which then represents a decimal point. A number may also have a power of ten suffixed in conventional exponential notation: an "E" (upper or lower case) followed optionally by a plus or minus sign then followed by one or more decimal digits defining the power of ten.

Numbers may have leading blanks (before and/or after the sign, if any) and may have trailing blanks. Blanks may not be embedded among the digits of a number or in the exponential part.

Examples:

```
'12'
'-17.9'
'127.0650'
'73e+128'
'  +  7.9E5  '
'0E000'
```

Note that the sequence -17.9 (without quotes) in an expression is not simply a number. It is a minus operator (which may be prefix minus if there is no term to the left of it) followed by a positive number. The result of the operation will be a number.

A *whole number* in REXX is a number that has a zero (or no) decimal part, and which would not normally be expressed by REXX in exponential notation – that is, it has no more digits before the decimal point than the current setting of NUMERIC DIGITS (the default is nine digits). See also page 137.

Implementation minimum: All implementations must support 9-digit arithmetic. In unavoidable cases this may be limited to integers only, and in this case the divide operator ("/") must not be supported. If exponents are supported in an implementation, then they must be supported for exponents whose absolute value is at least as large as the largest number that can be expressed as an exact integer in default precision, *i.e.*, 999999999.

Parentheses and operator precedence

Expression evaluation is from left to right; this is modified by parentheses and by operator precedence:

- When parentheses are encountered,[22] the entire sub-expression between the parentheses is evaluated immediately when the term is required.

- When the sequence

      $term_1$ $operator_1$ $term_2$ $operator_2$ $term_3$

  is encountered, and $operator_2$ has a higher precedence than $operator_1$, then the sub-expression ($term_2$ $operator_2$ $term_3$) is evaluated first. The same rule is applied repeatedly as necessary.

  Note, however, that individual terms are evaluated from left to right in the expression (that is, as soon as they are encountered). It is only the order of **operations** that is affected by the precedence rules.

For example, "*" (multiply) has a higher precedence than "+" (add), so 3+2*5 will evaluate to 13 (rather than the 25 that would result if strict left to right evaluation occurred). To force the addition to be performed before the

---

[22] Other than those that identify function calls – see below, on page 77.

multiplication the expression would be written $(3+2)*5$, where the first three tokens have been formed into a sub-expression by the addition of parentheses.

The order of precedence of the operators is (highest at the top):

Prefix operators

              +   -   ¬   \

Power operator

              **

Multiplication and division

              *   /   %   //

Addition and subtraction

              +   -

Concatenation

         (blank) || (abuttal)

Comparative operators

         =   ==   >   <   >=   ¬>   <<   \>>   *etc.*

And

              &

Or, exclusive or

              | &&

If, for example, the symbol A is a variable whose value is '3', and DAY is a variable with the value 'Monday' (others are uninitialized), then:

```
a+5                ==   '8'
a-4*2              ==   '-5'
a/2                ==   '1.5'
0.5**2             ==   '0.25'
(a+1)>7            ==   '0'              /* that is, False */
' '='              ==   '1'             /* that is, True  */
' '=='             ==   '0'             /* that is, False */
' '¬=='            ==   '1'             /* that is, True  */
(a+1)*3=12         ==   '1'             /* that is, True  */
'077'>'11'         ==   '1'             /* that is, True  */
'077'>>'11'        ==   '0'             /* that is, False */
'abc'>>'ab'        ==   '1'             /* that is, True  */
Today is day       ==   'TODAY IS Monday'
'If it is' day     ==   'If it is Monday'
substr(day,2,3)    ==   'ond'     /* Substr is a function */
'!'xxx'!'          ==   '!XXX!'
```

Note: The REXX order of precedence usually causes no difficulty, as it is the same as in conventional algebra and other computer languages. There are two differences from some common notations; the prefix minus operator always has a higher priority than the power operator, and power operators (like other operators) are evaluated left-to-right. Thus

```
-3**2        ==   9    /* not -9  */
-(2+1)**2    ==   9    /* not -9  */
2**2**3      ==   64   /* not 256 */
```

SECTION 4:   CLAUSES AND INSTRUCTIONS

Clauses (see page 18) may be classified as follows:

Null clauses

> A clause consisting of only blanks and/or comments is a *null clause* and is completely ignored by REXX (except that if it includes a comment it will be traced, if appropriate).

> **Note:** A null clause is not an instruction, so (for example) putting an extra semicolon after the THEN or ELSE in an IF instruction is not equivalent to putting a dummy instruction (as it would be in PL/I). The NOP instruction is provided for this purpose.

Labels

> A clause that consists of a single symbol followed by a colon is a *label*. The colon in this context implies a semicolon (clause separator), and so a label is a clause in its own right and no semicolon is required. Labels are used to identify the targets of CALL instructions, SIGNAL instructions, and internal function calls; and more than one label may precede any instruction. Labels are treated as null clauses, and may be traced selectively to aid debugging.

> Any number of successive clauses may be labels. This permits multiple labels before other clauses. Duplicate labels are permitted, but control will only pass to the first of any duplicates in a program. Others may be traced but cannot be used as a target of a CALL, SIGNAL, or function invocation.

Instructions

> An *instruction* consists of one or more clauses that describe some course of action to be taken by the language processor. Instructions may be either Assignments, Keyword Instructions, or Commands:

Assignments

> Single clauses with the form *symbol = expression* are instructions known as *assignments*. An assignment gives a variable a (new) value. See page 32.

Keyword Instructions

> A *keyword instruction* consists of one or more clauses, the first of which starts with a keyword that identifies the instruction. Keyword instructions control the external interfaces, the flow of control, and so on. Some keyword instructions (such as DO) can include nested instructions. See page 39.

Commands

Single clauses consisting of just an expression are instructions known as *commands*. The expression is evaluated and the result is passed as a command string to some external environment. See page 37.

SECTION 5: ASSIGNMENTS AND VARIABLES

A *variable* is a named object whose value may be changed during the course of execution of a REXX program. The process of changing the value of a variable is called *assigning* a new value to it. The value of a variable is a single character string, of any length, that may contain **any** characters.

Variables may be assigned a new value by the ARG, PARSE, or PULL instructions, but the most common way of changing the value of a variable is the assignment clause itself. Any clause of the form:

---

symbol = *expression* ;

---

is taken to be an *assignment*. The result of the expression becomes the new value of the variable named by the symbol to the left of the equals sign. The symbol is the *name* of the variable.

Example:

```
/* Next line gives FRED the value 'Frederic' */
fred='Frederic'
```

The symbol naming the variable cannot begin with a digit (0-9) or a period.[23]

Symbols may be used in an expression even if they have not been assigned a value, since they have a defined value at all times. When a variable has not been assigned a value it is *uninitialized*, and its value is the character(s) of the symbol itself, translated to upper case (unless it is a compound symbol, as described below, in which case its value is the derived name of the symbol).

Example:

```
/* If "freya" has not yet been assigned a value, */
/* then next line gives FRED the value 'FREYA'    */
fred=freya
```

The meaning of a symbol in REXX varies according to its context. When used as a term in an expression (rather than as a keyword of some kind, for example), symbols may be subdivided into four groups: *constant symbols*, *simple symbols*, *compound symbols*, and *stems*. *Constant symbols* are those that cannot

---

[23] Without this restriction on the first character of a variable name, it would be possible to redefine a number, in that for example the assignment "3=4;" would give a variable called "3" the value '4'.

be assigned a new value. *Simple symbols* may be used for variables where the name corresponds to a single value. *Compound symbols* and *stems* are used for more complex collections of variables, such as arrays and lists.

Constant symbols

The symbol starts with a digit (0-9) or a period.

The value of a constant symbol cannot be changed, and is simply the string consisting of the characters of the symbol with any alphabetic characters translated to upper case.

These are *constant symbols*:

```
77
827.53
.12345
12e5          /* Same as 12E5 */
3D
```

Simple symbols

The symbol itself does not contain any periods, and does not start with a digit (0-9).

By default its value is the characters of the symbol (translated to upper case). If the symbol has been assigned a value, it names a variable and its value is the value of that variable.

These are *simple symbols*:

```
FRED
Whatagoodidea!    /* Same as WHATAGOODIDEA! */
?12
```

Compound symbols

The symbol itself contains at least one period, and at least two other characters. It may not start with a digit or a period, and if there is only one period it may not be the last character.

The name begins with a *stem* (that part of the symbol up to and includ- ing the first period). This is followed by the *tail* – parts of the name (delimited by periods) that are constant symbols,[24] simple symbols, or null.

These are *compound symbols*:

```
fred.3
Array.I.J
AMESSY..One.2.
```

---

[24] Note that constant symbols with embedded signs cannot be used here, because with the stem prefixed the whole would not be a valid symbol.

Before the symbol is used (that is, at the time of reference), the values of any simple symbols in the tail ("I", "J", and "ONE" in the example) are substituted into the symbol, thus generating a new *derived name*. The value of a compound symbol is by default its derived name (used exactly as is), or (if it has been used as the target of an assignment) its value is the value of the variable named by the derived name.

The substitution into the symbol that takes place permits arbitrary indexing (subscripting) of collections of variables that have a common stem. Note that the values substituted may contain **any** characters (including periods and blanks). Substitution is only done once.

More formally, the *derived name* of a compound variable that is referenced by the symbol

$$s_0.s_1.s_2. \; \text{---} \; .s_n$$

is given by

$$d_0.v_1.v_2. \; \text{---} \; .v_n$$

where d_0 is the upper case form of the symbol s_0, and v_1 to v_n are the values of the constant or simple symbols s_1 through s_n. Any of the symbols s_1-s_n may be null. The values v_1-v_n may also be null and may contain **any** characters (in particular, lower case characters will not be translated to upper case, blanks will not be removed, and periods have no special significance).

Some examples follow in the form of a small extract from a REXX program:

```
a=3        /* Assigns '3' to the variable 'A'   */
b=4                 /*    '4'      to 'B'        */
c='Fred'            /*    'Fred'   to 'C'        */
a.b='Fred'          /*    'Fred'   to 'A.4'      */
a.fred=5            /*    '5'      to 'A.FRED'   */
a.c='Bill'          /*    'Bill'   to 'A.Fred'   */
c.c=a.fred          /*    '5'      to 'C.Fred'   */
x.a.b='Caver'       /*    'Caver'  to 'X.3.4'    */

say  a  b  c  a.a  a.b  a.c  c.a  a.fred x.a.4

/* Will display the string:                      */
/*     '3 4 Fred A.3 Fred Bill C.3 5 Caver'      */
```

Compound symbols may be used to set up arrays and lists of variables, in which the subscript is not necessarily numeric, and thus offer great scope for the creative programmer. A useful application is to set up an array in which the subscripts are taken from the value of one or more variables, so effecting a form of associative memory ("content addressable"). See the JUSTONE routine on page 5 for one example, and later in this section (page 35) for another.

Implementation minimum: Implementations should support variable names whose length, after substitution, may become at least 50 characters.

Stems

The symbol itself contains just one period, which is the last character. It may not start with a digit or a period.

These are *stems*:

```
fred.
A.
Woodstock.
```

By default, the value of a stem is the characters of its symbol, translated to upper case. If the symbol has been assigned a value, it names a variable and its value is the value of that variable.

Further, when a stem is used as the target of an assignment, **all possible** compound variables whose names begin with that stem are given the new value, whether they had a previous value or not. Following the assignment, a reference to any compound symbol with that stem will return the new value until another value is assigned to the stem or to the individual variable.

Example:

```
hole.   = "empty"
hole.19 = "full"

say  hole.1  hole.mouse  hole.19

/* Says "empty empty full" */
```

Thus a whole collection of variables may be given the same value.

Example:

```
total. = 0
do forever
    say "Enter an amount and a name:"
    pull amount name
    if datatype(amount)='CHAR' then leave
    total.name = total.name + amount
    end
```

(Another example may be found in Part 1 of this book, on page 5.)

Note: The value that has been assigned to the whole collection of variables can always be obtained by using the stem. However, this is not the same as using a compound variable whose derived name is the same as the stem.

Example:

```
total. = 0
null = ''
total.null = total.null + 5
say total. total.null                    /* says "0 5" */
```

Collections of variables, referred to by their stem, can also be manipulated by the DROP and PROCEDURE instructions. "DROP FRED." will drop all variables with that stem (see page 53), and "PROCEDURE EXPOSE FRED." will expose **all possible** variables with that stem (see page 65).

Notes:

1. When a variable is changed by the ARG, PARSE, or PULL instructions, the effect is identical to an assignment. A stem used in a parsing template will therefore set an entire collection of variables.

2. Since an expression may include the operator "=", and an instruction may consist purely of an expression (see next section), there is a potential ambiguity which is resolved by the following rule: any clause that starts with a symbol and whose second token is (or starts with) "=" is an assignment, rather than an expression. This is not a restriction, since the clause may be executed as a command in several ways, such as by putting a null string before the first name or by enclosing the first part of the expression in parentheses.

    Similarly, if a programmer unintentionally uses a REXX keyword as the variable name in an assignment, this should not cause confusion – for example the clause:

    ```
    address='10 Downing Street';
    ```

    would be an assignment, not an ADDRESS instruction.

3. The SYMBOL function (see page 108) may be used to test whether a symbol has been assigned a value. In addition, SIGNAL ON NOVALUE can be set to trap the use of any uninitialized variable (see page 145).

SECTION 6:   COMMANDS TO EXTERNAL ENVIRONMENTS

A *command* is a simple mechanism for sending a message to some functional unit external to a REXX program. It is usually a request for some service or action, and consists of a single character string. Many operating systems and other programs have a command language interface of this nature.

The system under which a REXX program runs will usually include at least one active environment for executing commands. One of these is selected by default on entry to a REXX program.   The active environment may be changed using the ADDRESS instruction, and the name of the currently selected environment may be found with the ADDRESS built-in function. Environments are defined externally to the REXX program by the underlying operating system.

Sending commands to the currently addressed environment may be achieved with a clause of the form:

---

expression ;

The expression is evaluated, resulting in a character string (which may be the null string) that is then submitted to the underlying system.

The underlying operating system will then obey the command (which may have side-effects such as placing data on the external data queue). It will eventually return control to REXX, after setting a *return code* (typically an integer, passed in an implementation-dependent way). REXX will place this return code in the special variable RC.

In addition to setting a return code, the underlying system may also indicate to the language processor whether an error or a failure occurred. An *error* in a command is a condition for which a program that uses that command would normally be expected to be prepared. (For example, a Locate command to an editor might report "requested string not found" as an error.) A command *failure* is a condition from which a program that uses that command would **not** normally be expected to recover (for example, if the command was not executable or could not be found).

Errors and failures in commands can directly affect REXX execution if a condition trap for ERROR or FAILURE is ON (see page 145). They may also cause the command to be traced if "TRACE Error" or "TRACE Failure" respectively are set.   "TRACE Normal" means the same as "TRACE Failure", and is the default – see page 73.

These matters are perhaps best illustrated with a specific example.

If the underlying system were the VM/CMS operating system, then the sequence

```
filename='CAVES'; filetype='VISITED'
'STATE' filename filetype
```

would result in the command string "STATE CAVES VISITED" being sub-mitted to VM/CMS. Of course, the simpler clause

```
'STATE CAVES VISITED'
```

would have the same effect in this case.

The operating system would then obey this command (which tests for the existence of the file CAVES VISITED), and on return the return code would be placed in the variable RC. RC would then normally have the value '0' if the file CAVES VISITED existed, or '28' if it did not. By convention in VM/CMS, a return code of 0 means successful completion, and a negative return code indicates a failure. Positive return codes usually indicate errors and often convey additional information, depending upon the command and the environment.

SECTION 7:   KEYWORD INSTRUCTIONS

A *keyword instruction* is one or more clauses, the first of which starts with a keyword that identifies the instruction. Some keyword instructions affect the flow of control; the remainder just provide services to the programmer. Some keyword instructions (such as DO) can include nested instructions. Appendix B, on page 171, shows an example of a REXX program using many of the instructions available.

In the syntax diagrams in this section (and, indeed, throughout the book), words (symbols) in capitals denote keywords or sub-keywords, and other words (such as *expression*) denote a collection of tokens as defined elsewhere. The brackets [and] delimit optional (and possibly alternative) parts of the instructions, whereas the braces { and } indicate that one of a number of alternatives must be selected. An ellipsis following a bracket indicates that that bracketed part of the clause may optionally be repeated.

Note that the keywords and sub-keywords in the syntax diagrams are not case dependent: the symbols "if" "If" and "iF" would all identify the instruction shown below as "IF". Note also that most of the clause delimiters (;) shown may usually be omitted as they will be implied by the end of a line.

Appendix A, on page 165, collects together the syntax diagrams for ease of reference.

As indicated earlier, a keyword instruction is recognized **only** if its keyword is the first token in a clause, and if the second token neither starts with an = character (implying an assignment) nor a colon (implying a label). The keywords ELSE, END, OTHERWISE, THEN, and WHEN are recognized in the same situation.[25] It is an error if these keywords are found other than in their correct position in a DO, IF, or SELECT instruction. Note that any clause that starts with a keyword defined by REXX cannot be a command, so, for example, the clause

```
arg(fred) rest
```

is an ARG keyword instruction, not a command that starts with a call to the ARG built-in function.

Other than in the context just described, keywords are not reserved and may be used as labels or as the names of variables (though this is not recommended).

Certain other keywords, known as *sub-keywords*, may be reserved within the clauses of individual instructions – for example the symbols TO and WHILE in the DO instruction. (For details, refer to the description of each instruction.) For a general discussion on reserved words, see page 154.

---

[25] The keyword THEN may also be recognized in the body of an IF or WHEN clause.

Blanks adjacent to keywords have no effect other than that of separating the keyword from the subsequent token. For example, this applies to the blanks next to the sub-keyword WHILE in

```
do while   a=3
```

Here at least one blank was required to separate the symbols forming the keywords and variable name. However the blank following the WHILE is not necessary in

```
do while 'Me'=a
```

though it does aid readability.

ADDRESS

$$\text{ADDRESS} \begin{bmatrix} environment\ [exprc] \\ [\text{VALUE}]\ exprv \end{bmatrix};$$

where *environment* is a symbol or literal string, which is taken as a constant, and *exprc* and *exprv* are *expressions*.

The ADDRESS instruction is used to effect a temporary or permanent change to the destination of commands. Commands are strings sent to an external environment, and may be sent by clauses consisting of just an expression (see page 37) as well as by the ADDRESS instruction.

To send a single command to a specified environment, an environment name followed by an expression, *exprc*, is given. The expression is evaluated, and the resulting command string is submitted to the given environment. After execution of the command the previously selected environment will be unchanged.

Example:

```
address DOS 'DIR MDV1.ALL'
```

would send the command "DIR MDV1.ALL" to the environment called DOS. The special variable RC is set, just as it would be for other commands (see page 37). Errors and failures in commands executed in this way are trapped or traced as usual.

If only an environment name is specified, a new environment for commands is selected. All following commands will be routed to the new command environment, until the next ADDRESS instruction is executed. The previously selected environment is saved.

Example:

```
address CMS       /* Send following commands to CMS */
'STATE PROFILE EXEC'
if rc=0 then 'COPY PROFILE EXEC A TEMP = ='
address XEDIT     /* And now all commands to XEDIT */
```

Similarly, the VALUE form may be used to select a new environment – here the expression *exprv* (which of course may be simply a reference to a variable) is evaluated, and the result forms the name of the new environment. The sub-keyword VALUE may be omitted if the expression does not begin with a symbol or literal string (*i.e.*, if it starts with a special character, such as an operator character or parenthesis).

If ADDRESS is specified without either an environment name or an expression, then commands will be routed back to the environment that was selected before the previous lasting change of environment was made (and the current environment name is saved). Repeated execution of just "ADDRESS" will therefore switch the command destination between two alternative environments.

The two environment names maintained by REXX are automatically saved across internal subroutine and function calls. See the CALL instruction (page 43) for more details.

The current ADDRESS setting may be retrieved using the ADDRESS built-in function. See page 82.

Note: The null string may be used as an environment name. Like all environment names, its meaning (if any) is defined by the underlying operating system.

ARG

ARG [*template*];

where *template* is a list of symbols separated by blanks and/or patterns.

ARG is used to retrieve the argument string or strings provided to a program or internal routine and put them into variables. It is just a shorter form of the instruction

```
PARSE UPPER ARG [template];
```

Unless a subroutine or internal function is being executed, the strings passed as parameters to the program will be translated to upper case and then parsed into variables according to the rules described in the section on parsing (page 118). Use the PARSE ARG instruction if upper case translation is not desired.

If a subroutine or internal function is being executed, then the data used will be the argument string(s) passed to the routine.

The ARG (and PARSE ARG) instructions may be executed repeatedly (typically with different templates) and will always parse the same current data. There are no restrictions on the length or content of the data parsed except those imposed by the caller.

Example:

```
/* String passed to FRED EXEC is 'Easy Rider'   */

arg adjective noun .

/* Now:   ADJECTIVE contains 'EASY'             */
/*        NOUN      contains 'RIDER'            */
```

If more than one string is expected to be available to the program or routine, then each may be selected in turn by using a comma in the parsing template.

Example:

```
/* Function is invoked by  FRED('Ogof X',1,5)   */

Fred:  arg string, num1, num2

/* Now:   STRING contains 'OGOF X'              */
/*        NUM1   contains '1'                   */
/*        NUM2   contains '5'                   */
```

The argument string(s) to a REXX program or internal routine may also be retrieved or checked by using the ARG built-in function. See page 83.

Note: A description of the source of the data being interpreted is also made available on entry to the program. See the PARSE instruction (SOURCE option) on page 63 for details.

CALL

$$
\text{CALL} \quad
\begin{cases}
name \ [expression] \ [\,, \ [expression]\,] \dots \\
\text{ON } condition \ [\text{NAME } trapname] \\
\text{OFF } condition
\end{cases} \ ;
$$

where *name* is a symbol or literal string which is taken as a constant, and *condition* and *trapname* are single symbols which are taken as constants.

CALL is used to invoke a routine, or (if ON or OFF is specified) may be used to control the trapping of certain conditions (see page 145).

If neither ON nor OFF is specified, CALL invokes a *subroutine* which may be an internal routine, a built-in function, or an external routine. The subroutine may optionally return a result, and so the CALL instruction is functionally identical to the clause

```
result=name([expression] [,[expression]]...);
```

except that the variable RESULT will become uninitialized if no result is returned by the routine invoked.

The *name* given in the CALL instruction must be a symbol, which is treated literally, or a literal string. If a literal string is used for the name (that is, the name is specified in quotes) the search for internal labels is bypassed, and only a built-in function or an external routine will be invoked. Note that the names of built-in functions (and often the names of external routines too) are in upper case, and hence the name in the literal string should be in upper case.

The expressions following the *name* are evaluated in order from left to right, and form the argument string(s) during execution of the routine. The ARG and PARSE ARG instructions (and the ARG built-in function) will access these strings rather than any active previously, until control returns to the CALL instruction. Expressions may be omitted, if appropriate, by including "extra" commas.

The CALL then causes a branch to the routine called *name* using exactly the same mechanism as function calls. Therefore the CALL instruction may be used to invoke internal routines, external routines, or even built-in functions. The order of search for these routines is described in the section on functions (page 79), but briefly is as follows:

Internal (Unless the routine name is specified in quotes.) Internal routines are sequences of REXX instructions inside the same program, which start at the label that matches the symbol following the keyword CALL. A form of multi-way call to internal routines can be effected with the aid of the SIGNAL instruction (see page 73). The RETURN instruction is used to complete the execution of an internal routine.

Built-in These are routines defined as part of the language. Most are usually called as functions, and all return a string that contains the result of the routine. (See page 81.)

External It is usually possible to write or make use of routines that are external to a program. These external routines may be written in any language (including REXX) which supports the implementation-dependent interfaces used by the REXX language processor to invoke them. If the external routine is written in REXX then any argument strings may be retrieved in the usual way by using the ARG or PARSE ARG instructions (or the ARG built-in function).

During execution of an internal routine, all variables previously known are normally accessible. However, the PROCEDURE instruction may be used to set up a local variables environment to protect the subroutine and caller from each other. The EXPOSE option on the PROCEDURE instruction may further be used to expose selected variables to a routine.[26]

When control reaches an internal routine, the line number of the CALL instruction is assigned to the special variable SIGL (in the caller's variable environment). This can be used as an aid to debugging, as it may be used to determine the source of a call to a routine.[27]

Eventually the subroutine should execute a RETURN instruction, and at that point control will return to the original CALL instruction for completion. If the RETURN instruction specified an expression, then the variable RESULT will be set to the value of that expression. Otherwise the variable RESULT is dropped (becomes uninitialized).

Internal routines may include calls to other internal routines. If a routine calls itself (either directly, or indirectly via one or more other routines), this is termed a *recursive* call.

---

[26] Calling an external REXX program as a subroutine is similar to calling an internal routine. The external routine is however an implicit PROCEDURE in that all the caller's variables are always hidden, and the state of internal values (NUMERIC settings, *etc.*) starts with their defaults (rather than inheriting those of the caller). In addition, EXIT may be used to return from the routine.

[27] Note that if the internal routine uses the PROCEDURE instruction then it will need to EXPOSE SIGL to get access to the line number of the CALL.

Example:

FACTOR1

```
/* Example of recursive subroutine execution. */
arg x
call factorial x
say x'! =' result
exit

Factorial: procedure      /* calculate factorial by.. */
   arg n                   /*  .. recursive invocation. */
   if n=0 then return 1
   call factorial n-1
   return result*n
```

(This example may be compared with the example on page 79 in which a similar factorial routine is invoked as a function.)

State saved across calls:

During internal subroutine (and function) execution the following pieces of information are automatically saved and are then restored upon return from the routine.

- **The state of DO loops and other structures.** Executing a SIGNAL while within a subroutine is "safe" in that DO loops *etc.* that were active when the routine was called are not deactivated (but those active within the current routine will be).

- **NUMERIC settings** (The DIGITS, FUZZ, and FORM of arithmetic operations described on page 59.) A subroutine may therefore set the precision *etc.* that it needs to use without fear of affecting the caller.

- **ADDRESS settings** (The current and saved destinations for commands – see the ADDRESS instruction on page 40.)

- **Condition traps** (Described on page 145). CALL ON, CALL OFF, SIGNAL ON, and SIGNAL OFF may be used in a subroutine without affecting the state of the condition traps or trap names set up by the caller.

- **Condition information** The information returned by the CONDITION built-in function (see pages 89 and 149).

- **OPTIONS settings** (Some or all of the options set by the OPTIONS instruction – see page 61.) Note that options settings and their meaning are implementation dependent, and they are not necessarily saved across calls.

- **Elapsed time clocks**. A subroutine inherits the elapsed time clock from its caller (see the TIME function on page 108), but since the time clock is saved across routine calls a subroutine or internal function may independently restart and use the clock without affecting its caller. For the same reason, a clock started within an internal routine is not available to the caller.

• **Trace settings.** Once a subroutine is debugged, you may insert a "TRACE Normal" at the beginning of it, and this will not affect the tracing of the caller. Conversely, if you only wish to debug a subroutine, you could insert a "TRACE Results" at the start – tracing will automatically be restored to the conditions at entry (for example, "Off") upon return. Interactive tracing state is included in the saved setting.

Implementation minimum: Nesting of control structures (which includes internal routine calls) should be allowed up to a depth of at least 100.

Implementation minimum: At least 10 argument expressions should be allowed on a CALL instruction.

DO

DO [*repetitor*] [*conditional*] ;
    [*instructionlist*]
    END [*symbol*] ;

where *repetitor* is one of

    name = *expri* [TO *exprt*] [BY *exprb*] [FOR *exprf*]
    exprr
    FOREVER

and *conditional* is either of

    WHILE *exprw*
    UNTIL *expru*

and *instructionlist* is

    any sequence of *instructions*

and *expri*, *exprt*, *exprb*, *exprf*, *exprr*, *exprw*, and *expru* are *expressions*.

The DO instruction is used to group instructions together and optionally to execute them repetitively. During repetitive execution, a control variable, *name*, may be stepped through some series of values.

Syntax notes:

- *expri*, *exprt*, *exprb*, *exprf*, and *exprr* may be any expression that evaluates to a number. If necessary, the number will be rounded according to the setting of NUMERIC DIGITS before it is used. *exprr* and *exprf* are further restricted to result in a non-negative whole number.

- *exprw* or *expru* may be any expression that evaluates to '1' or '0'.

- The TO, BY, and FOR phrases may be in any order, if used, and will be evaluated in the order they are written.

- Any instruction is allowed in *instructionlist*, including assignments, commands, and keyword instructions (including any of the more complex constructions such as IF, SELECT, or the DO instruction itself).

- The sub-keywords WHILE and UNTIL are reserved within a DO instruction, in that they cannot be used as symbols in any of the expressions. Similarly, TO, BY, and FOR cannot be used in *expri*, *exprt*, *exprb*, or *exprf*. FOREVER is also reserved, but only if it immediately follows the keyword DO.

- *exprb* defaults to '1', if relevant.

DO is the most complicated of the REXX keyword instructions. It can be treated as a simple grouping construct, a pre-determined repetitive loop, and as a loop with a bounding condition that is recalculated on each iteration.

Simple DO group

If neither *repetitor* nor *conditional* is given, then the construct merely groups a number of instructions together: these are executed once.

Example:

```
/* The two instructions between DO and END will both */
/* be executed if A has the value 3.                 */
if a=3 then do
  a=a+2
  say 'Smile!'
  end
```

Repetitive DO loops

If either *repetitor* or *conditional* is given, the group of instructions forms a *repetitive DO loop,* and the instruction list is executed according to any *repetitor phrase*, optionally modified by a *conditional phrase*.

Simple repetitive loops

> If the *repetitor* is FOREVER (or if no *repetitor* is given, but there is a *conditional*, see below), then the instruction list will nominally be executed "for ever", that is, until the condition is satisfied or a LEAVE, SIGNAL, EXIT, or RETURN instruction is executed.

Example:

```
/* This displays "Go caving!" at least once */
do forever
   say 'Go caving!'
   if random(5)=1 then leave
   end
```

Alternatively, in the numeric form of *repetitor*, the expression *exprr* is evaluated immediately (and must result in a whole number that is zero or positive), and the loop is then executed that many times:

Example:

```
/* This displays "Hello" five times */
do 5
   say 'Hello'
   end
```

Note that, similar to the distinction between a command and an assignment, if the first token of *exprr* is a symbol and the second token is (or starts with) an "=", then the controlled form of repetitor is expected.

Controlled repetitive loops

A *controlled repetitive loop* specifies a control variable, *name*, which is given an initial value (the result of *expri*, formatted as though '0' had been added) before the first execution of the instruction list. The variable is then stepped (by adding the result of *exprb*) before the second and subsequent times that the instruction list is executed.

The instruction list is executed repeatedly while the end condition (determined by the result of *exprt*) is not met. If *exprb* is positive or zero, then the loop will be terminated when *name* is greater than the result of *exprt*. If negative, then the loop will be terminated when *name* is less than the result of *exprt*.

The expressions *expri*, *exprt*, and *exprb* must result in numbers. They are evaluated once only, before the loop begins and before the control variable is set to its initial value. The default value for *exprb* is 1. If no *exprt* is given then the loop will execute indefinitely unless it is terminated by some other condition.

Example:

```
do i=3 to -2 by -1
  say i
  end
/* Would display: 3, 2, 1, 0, -1, -2 */
```

Note that the numbers do not have to be whole numbers:

Example:

```
x=0.3
do y=x to x+4 by 0.7
  say y
  end
/* Would display: 0.3, 1.0, 1.7, 2.4, 3.1, 3.8 */
```

The control variable may be altered within the loop, and this may affect the iteration of the loop. Altering the value of the control variable in this way is normally considered to be suspect programming practice, though it may be appropriate in certain circumstances.

Note that the end condition is tested at the start of each iteration (and after the control variable is stepped, on the second and subsequent iterations). It is therefore possible for the instruction list to be skipped entirely if the end condition is met immediately.

Note also that the control variable is referenced by name. If (for example) the compound name "A.I" was used for the control variable, then altering "I" within the loop will cause a change in the control variable.

The execution of a controlled loop may further be bounded by a FOR phrase. In this case, *exprf* must be given and must evaluate to a non-negative whole number. This acts just like the repetition count in a simple repetitive loop, and sets a limit to the number of iterations around the loop if it is not terminated by some other condition. Like the TO and BY expressions it is evaluated once only, when the DO instruction is first executed and before the control variable is given its initial value. Like the TO condition, the FOR count is checked at the start of each iteration.

Example:

```
do y=0.3 to 4.3 by 0.7 for 3
   say y
   end
/* Would display: 0.3, 1.0, 1.7 */
```

In a controlled loop, a symbol that describes the control variable may be specified on the END clause. REXX will then check that this symbol exactly matches the *name* of the control variable in the DO clause (in all respects except case). Note that no substitution for compound variables is carried out. If the symbol does not match, then the program is in error – this enables the nesting of loops to be checked automatically.

Example:

```
do k=1 to 10
   . . .
   . . .
   end k   /* Checks this is the END for K loop */
```

Note: The values taken by the control variable may be affected by the NUMERIC settings, since normal REXX arithmetic rules apply to the computation of stepping the control variable.

Conditional phrases (WHILE and UNTIL)

Any of the forms of *repetitor* (none, FOREVER, numeric, or controlled) can be followed by a *conditional* phrase which may cause termination of the loop. If WHILE or UNTIL is specified, the expression following it is evaluated each time around the loop using the latest values of all variables (and must evaluate to either '0' or '1'), and the instruction list will be repeatedly executed either while the result is '1', or until the result is '1'.

For a "WHILE" loop, the condition is evaluated before the instruction list is executed, and for an "UNTIL" loop the condition is evaluated after the instruction list is executed − before the control variable has been stepped.

Example:

```
do i=1 to 10 by 2 until i>6
  say i
  end
/* Would display: 1, 3, 5, 7 */
```

Note that the execution of repetitive loops may also be modified by using the LEAVE or ITERATE instructions.

Programmer's model – how a typical DO loop is executed

This model forms part of the definition of the DO instruction.

For the following DO:

```
DO name=expri TO exprt BY exprb WHILE exprw
   ....
   instruction list
   ....
   END
```

REXX will execute the following:[28]

```
        $tempi=expri      /* ($variables are internal and   */
        $tempt=exprt      /*   are not accessible.)          */
        $tempb=exprb
        name=$tempi+0
        Transfer control to label $start

 $loop:
        /* An UNTIL expression would be tested here, with: */
        /* if expru then leave                             */
        name=name + $tempb
 $start:
        if name > $tempt then leave  /* leave quits a loop */
        /* A FOR count would be checked here               */
        if ¬exprw then leave
           ....
           instruction list
           ....
        Transfer control to label $loop
```

Note: This example is for *exprb* >= 0. For negative *exprb*, the test at the start of the loop would be "<" rather than ">".

---

[28] Note that the only action directly corresponding to the END clause is an upwards transfer of control.

DROP

DROP *variablelist* ;

where *variablelist* is one or more symbols (optionally enclosed in parentheses) separated by blanks.

DROP is used to "un-assign" variables. It restores them to their original uninitialized state.

The symbols in *variablelist* must be valid variable names. Each variable named will be dropped from the collection of known variables, unless the variable name is enclosed in parentheses. In this latter case, a *variable reference*, the parentheses enclose a single name (blanks are not necessary either inside or outside the parentheses, but may be added if desired), and the value of the variable is used as a subsidiary variable list which must follow the same rules as the original list except that no parentheses are allowed.[29]

The variables named in the original list (outside of parentheses) or in subsidiary lists are dropped in sequence from left to right (with variables in subsidiary lists dropped as soon as the value of the list variable has been found). It is not an error to specify a name more than once, or to DROP a variable that is not known. If an exposed variable is named (see the PROCEDURE instruction on page 65), then the variable owned by the original caller will be dropped.

Examples:

```
j=4
drop  a x.3 x.j
/* would reset the variables: "A", "X.3", and "X.4"   */
/* A reference to them now returns their derived name */

mylist='a b c'
drop (mylist) d
/* would reset the variables: "A", "B", "C", and "D"   */
```

If a variable specified is the stem of a compound variable (*i.e.*, it is a symbol that contains only one period, as the last character), then all variables starting with that stem are dropped.

Example:

```
drop  x.
/* resets all variables whose names start with "X." */
```

---

[29] That is, it is a list of symbols that must be valid variable names, separated by blanks. Leading and trailing blanks are allowed.

EXIT

```
EXIT [expression];
```

EXIT is used to unconditionally leave a program, and optionally return a character string to the caller. The program is terminated immediately, even if an internal routine is currently being executed. If no internal routine is active, then RETURN (see page 69) and EXIT are identical in their effect on the program that is being executed.

If an expression is given, it is evaluated and the string resulting from the evaluation is then passed back to the caller when the program terminates. If no expression is given, no character string is passed back to the caller.

Example:

```
j=3
exit j*4
/* Would exit with the string '12' */
```

"Running off the end" of a program is always equivalent to the instruction "EXIT;", in that it terminates the whole program and returns no result string.

IF

```
IF expression [;] THEN [;] instruction [ELSE [;] instruction]
```

The IF construct is used to conditionally execute an instruction or group of instructions. It can also be used to select between two alternatives.

The expression is evaluated and must result in '0' or '1'. If the result was '1' then the instruction after the THEN is executed. If the result was '0' and an ELSE was given then the instruction after the ELSE is executed.

Example:

```
if answer='YES' then say 'OK!'
                else say 'Why not?'
```

Remember that if the ELSE clause is on the same line as the last clause of the THEN part, then you need a semicolon to terminate that clause.

Example:

```
if answer='YES' then say 'OK!';  else say 'Why not?'
```

The ELSE binds to the nearest IF at the same level. This means that any IF that is used as the instruction following the THEN in an IF construct that has an ELSE clause, must itself have an ELSE clause (which may be followed by the dummy instruction, NOP).

Example:

```
if answer='YES' then if name='FRED' then say 'OK, Fred.'
                                     else say 'OK.'
                 else say 'Why not?'
```

Notes:

1. An *instruction* may be any assignment, command, or keyword instruction, including any of the more complex constructions such as DO and SELECT and the IF instruction itself. A null clause is not an instruction, however, so putting an extra semicolon (or label) after the THEN or ELSE is not equivalent to putting a dummy instruction (as it would be in PL/I). The NOP instruction is provided for this purpose.

2. The keyword THEN is treated specially, in that it need not start a clause. This allows the expression on the IF clause to be terminated by the THEN, without a ";" being required – were this not so, people used to other computer languages would experience considerable difficulties. Hence the symbol THEN cannot be used within the expression.

INTERPRET

INTERPRET *expression* ;

INTERPRET is used to execute instructions that have been built dynamically by evaluating an expression (in contrast to those that already exist in the program).

The expression is evaluated, and will then be executed (interpreted) just as though the resulting string were a line inserted into the program (and bracketed by a DO; and an END;).

Any instructions (including INTERPRET instructions) are allowed, but note that constructions such as DO...END and SELECT...END must be complete. For example, a string of instructions being interpreted cannot contain a LEAVE or ITERATE instruction (valid only within a repetitive DO loop) unless it also contains the whole repetitive DO...END construct. Label clauses are not permitted in the interpreted character string.

A semicolon is implied at the end of the expression during execution, if one was not supplied.

Example:

```
data='FRED'
interpret data '= 4'
/* Will a) build the string  "FRED = 4"          */
/*      b) execute  "FRED = 4;"                   */
/* Thus the variable FRED will be set to '4'      */
```

Note: If you are new to the concept of the INTERPRET instruction and are getting results that you do not understand, then you may find that executing it with "TRACE R" or "TRACE I" set is helpful.

Example:

The program:

```
/* Here we have a small program. */     trace inter
name='Kitt'
indirect='name'
interpret 'say "Hello"' indirect'"!"'
```

when run gives the trace:

```
        2 *-* name='Kitt'
          >L>    "Kitt"
        3 *-* indirect='name'
          >L>    "name"
        4 *-* interpret 'say "Hello"' indirect'"!"'
          >L>    "say "Hello""
          >V>    "name"
          >O>    "say "Hello" name"
          >L>    ""!""
          >O>    "say "Hello" name"!""
          *-*  say "Hello" name"!"
          >L>     "Hello"
          >V>     "Kitt"
          >O>     "Hello Kitt"
          >L>     "!"
          >O>     "Hello Kitt!"
Hello Kitt!
```

Here, as shown in the trace, lines 2 and 3 set the variables used in line 4. Execution of line 4 then proceeds in two stages. First the string to be interpreted is built up, using a literal string, a variable (INDIRECT), and another literal string. The resulting pure character string is then interpreted, just as though it were actually part of the original program. Since it is a new clause, it is traced as such (the second "*-*" trace flag under line 4) and is then executed. Again a literal string is concatenated to the value of a variable (NAME) and another literal string, and the final result ("Hello Kitt!") is then displayed.

For many purposes, the VALUE function (see page 112) may be used instead of the INTERPRET instruction. Line 4 in the last example could have been replaced by:

```
say "Hello" value(indirect)"!"
```

INTERPRET is usually required only in special cases such as when more than one instruction is to be interpreted at once, or when an expression is to be evaluated dynamically (as in the SHOWME program on page 6).

ITERATE

ITERATE [*name*];

where *name* is a symbol, taken as a constant.

ITERATE alters the flow of control within a repetitive DO loop (*i.e.*, any DO construct other than that with a plain DO).

Execution of the instruction list stops, and control is passed back up to the DO clause just as though the END clause had been encountered. The control variable (if any) is then stepped (iterated) as normal and the instruction list is executed again, unless the loop is terminated by the DO clause.

If no *name* is specified, then ITERATE will step the innermost active repetitive loop. If a *name* is specified, then it must be the name of the control variable of a currently active loop (which may be the innermost), and this is the loop that is iterated. Any active loops inside the one selected for iteration are terminated (as though by a LEAVE instruction).

Example:

```
do i=1 to 4
  if i=2 then iterate
  say i
  end
/* Would display the numbers:  1, 3, 4  */
```

Notes:

1.   The *name* symbol, if specified, must exactly match the symbol naming the control variable in the DO clause (in all respects except case). No substitution for compound variables is carried out when the comparison is made.

2.   A loop is active if it is currently being executed. If a subroutine is called (or if an INTERPRET instruction is executed) during execution of a loop, then the loop becomes inactive until the subroutine has returned or the INTERPRET instruction has completed. ITERATE cannot be used to step an inactive loop.

3.   If more than one active loop uses the same control variable, then the innermost will be the one selected by the ITERATE.

LEAVE

> LEAVE [*name*] ;
>
> where *name* is a symbol, taken as a constant.

LEAVE causes immediate exit from one or more repetitive DO loops (*i.e.*, any DO construct other than that with a plain DO).

Execution of the instruction list is terminated, and control is passed to the instruction following the END clause, just as though the END clause had been encountered and the termination condition had been met normally, except that on exit the control variable (if any) will contain the value it had when the LEAVE instruction was executed.

If no *name* is specified, then LEAVE will terminate the innermost active repetitive loop. If a *name* is specified, then it must be the name of the control variable of a currently active loop (which may be the innermost), and that loop (and any active loops inside it) is then terminated. Control then passes to the clause following the END that matches the DO clause of the selected loop.

Example:

```
do i=1 to 5
  say i
  if i=3 then leave
  end
/* Would display the numbers:  1, 2, 3  */
```

Notes:

1.   The *name* symbol, if specified, must exactly match the symbol naming the control variable in the DO clause (in all respects except case). No substitution for compound variables is carried out when the comparison is made.

2.   A loop is active if it is currently being executed. If a subroutine is called (or if an INTERPRET instruction is executed) during execution of a loop, then the loop becomes inactive until the subroutine has returned or the INTERPRET instruction has completed. LEAVE cannot be used to terminate an inactive loop.

3.   If more than one active loop uses the same control variable, then the innermost will be the one selected by the LEAVE.

NOP

```
NOP ;
```

NOP is a dummy instruction that has no effect. It can be useful as the target
of a THEN or ELSE clause.

Example:

```
select
  when a=b then nop              /* Do nothing */
  when a>b then say 'A > B'
  otherwise     say 'A < B'
  end
```

Note: Putting an extra semicolon instead of the NOP would merely insert a
null clause, which would just be ignored by REXX. The second WHEN clause
would then immediately follow the THEN, and hence would be treated as a
syntax error. NOP is a true instruction, however, and is therefore a valid
target for the THEN clause.

NUMERIC

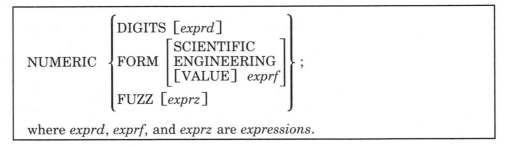

where *exprd*, *exprf*, and *exprz* are *expressions*.

The NUMERIC instruction is used to change the way in which arithmetic
operations are carried out. The effects of this instruction are described in
more detail on pages 127-138.

NUMERIC DIGITS

> controls the precision under which arithmetic operations and arithmetic
> built-in functions will be evaluated – see pages 129 and 81.   If no
> expression *exprd* is given then the default value of 9 is used. Otherwise
> the result of the expression is rounded, if necessary, according to the
> current setting of NUMERIC DIGITS before it is used. The value used
> must be a positive whole number that is larger than the current
> NUMERIC FUZZ setting.

> There is normally no limit to the value for NUMERIC DIGITS (except
> the constraints imposed by the amount of storage and other resources

available) but note that high precisions are likely to be expensive in processing time. It is recommended that the default value be used wherever possible.

Note that small values of NUMERIC DIGITS (for example, values less than 6) are generally only useful for specialized applications. The setting of NUMERIC DIGITS affects all computations, so even the operation of loops may be affected by rounding if small values are used.

If an implementation does not support a requested value of DIGITS then the NUMERIC DIGITS instruction will fail (and may, as usual, be trapped using SIGNAL ON SYNTAX). The current setting of NUMERIC DIGITS may be retrieved with the DIGITS built-in function – see page 94.

NUMERIC FORM

controls which form of exponential notation is to be used by REXX for the results of operations and arithmetic built-in functions. This may be either *scientific* (in which case only one, non-zero, digit will appear before the decimal point), or *engineering* (in which case the power of ten will always be a multiple of three). See page 136 for examples. The default is scientific.

The form is set either directly by the sub-keywords SCIENTIFIC or ENGINEERING, or is taken from the result of evaluating the expression, *exprf*, that follows VALUE. The result in this case must be either 'SCIENTIFIC' or 'ENGINEERING'. The sub-keyword VALUE may be omitted if the expression does not begin with a symbol or a literal string (*i.e.*, if it starts with a special character, such as an operator character or parenthesis).

The current setting of NUMERIC FORM may be retrieved with the FORM built-in function – see page 96. The FORM option may not be supported by all implementations. If it is not supported, the instruction will fail.

NUMERIC FUZZ

controls how many digits, at full precision, will be ignored during a numeric comparison – see page 135. If no expression *exprz* is given then the default value of 0 is used. Otherwise the result of the expression is rounded, if necessary, according to the current setting of NUMERIC DIGITS before it is used. The value used must be zero or a positive whole number that is smaller than the current NUMERIC DIGITS setting.

The effect of NUMERIC FUZZ is to temporarily reduce the value of NUMERIC DIGITS by the NUMERIC FUZZ value during every numeric comparison, so that the numbers are subtracted under a precision of DIGITS minus FUZZ digits during the comparison and are then compared with 0.

The current setting of NUMERIC FUZZ may be retrieved with the FUZZ built-in function – see page 97. The FUZZ option may not be supported by all implementations. If it is not supported, the instruction will fail.

Note: The three numeric settings are automatically saved across internal subroutine and function calls. See the CALL instruction (page 43) for more details.

OPTIONS

OPTIONS *expression* ;

The OPTIONS instruction is used to pass special requests to the language processor (for example, an interpreter or compiler).

The expression is evaluated, and individual words in the result that are meaningful to the language processor will be obeyed (these might control optimizations, enforce standards, enable implementation-dependent features, *etc.*). Words in the result that are not recognized will be ignored (they are assumed to be instructions to a different language processor).

For example:

```
options 'Speed Notrace 4.00'
```

might tell a compiler to optimize for speed, that no tracing will be used in this program, and that the rules for version 4.00 of the language definition should be enforced. A processor that did not recognize any of the words would ignore them.

Note: Some or all of the options set by the OPTIONS instruction may be automatically saved across internal subroutine and function calls, in a manner appropriate to the option and language processor. See page 43 for information on subroutine calls.

PARSE

$$
\text{PARSE [UPPER]} \left\{ \begin{array}{l} \text{ARG} \\ \text{LINEIN} \\ \text{PULL} \\ \text{SOURCE} \\ \text{VALUE } [\textit{expression}] \text{ WITH} \\ \text{VAR } \textit{name} \\ \text{VERSION} \end{array} \right\} \; [\textit{template}] \; ;
$$

where *template* is a list of symbols separated by blanks and/or patterns.

The PARSE instruction is used to assign data (from various sources) to one or more variables according to the rules and templates described in the section on parsing (page 118).

If UPPER is specified, then any character strings to be parsed are first translated to upper case. Otherwise no translation takes place during the parsing.

If no template is given, then no variables will be set but action will be taken to get the data ready for parsing if necessary. Thus for PARSE LINEIN and PARSE PULL a line will be removed from the appropriate character stream or data queue, for PARSE VALUE the expression will be evaluated, and for PARSE VAR the variable will be checked to ensure that it has a value.

The following list describes the data used for each variant of the PARSE instruction.

For PARSE ARG

> The string(s) passed to the program, subroutine, or function as the input arguments are parsed. (See the ARG instruction on page 42 for details and examples.)
>
> The argument string(s) to a REXX program may also be retrieved or checked by using the ARG built-in function. See page 83.

For PARSE LINEIN

> The next line from the default character input stream is parsed. (See page 139 for a discussion of the REXX input/output model.) PARSE LINEIN is a shorter form of the instruction
>
> ```
> PARSE VALUE LINEIN() WITH [template];
> ```
>
> See page 99 for a description of the LINEIN function. If no line is available, program execution will normally pause until a line is complete. Note that PARSE LINEIN should only be used when direct access to the character input stream is necessary. Normal line-by-line dialogue with

the user should be carried out with the PULL or PARSE PULL instructions, to maintain generality and programmability.

The number of lines available in the default character input stream may be found with the LINES built-in function. See page 101.

As an example, under the VM/CMS operating system, PARSE LINEIN will read directly from the terminal input buffer (as opposed to the program stack). If the input buffer is empty, then a console read results.

For PARSE PULL

The next string from the external data queue is parsed. (See page 139 for a discussion of the REXX input/output model.) This queue is implementation defined, but will at least support the ability to save a series of arbitrary data strings of reasonable length. If the external data queue is empty, lines will be read from the default character input stream, and the program will pause if necessary until a line is complete.

Strings can be added to the head or tail of the queue using the PUSH and QUEUE instructions respectively. The queue may also be altered by other programs in the system, and may be usable as a means of communication between programs. See also the PULL instruction, on page 67.

The number of lines currently in the data queue may be found with the QUEUED built-in function. See page 103.

As an example, under VM/CMS, PULL and PARSE PULL read from the program stack. If that is empty, they read from the terminal input buffer.

For PARSE SOURCE

The character string parsed describes the source of the program being executed in some implementation-dependent way. The string is fixed (will not change) during execution of the program. The first word will identify the system or implementation under which execution is progressing, the second should state how the program was invoked, and the remainder is entirely implementation-dependent but would normally include the full name of the program.

For example, under VM/CMS, the string contains the characters "CMS", followed by either "COMMAND", "FUNCTION", or "SUBROUTINE" depending on whether the program was invoked as some kind of command (for example, an Exec or an editor Macro), or from a function call in an expression, or via the CALL instruction. These two words are followed by the program filename, filetype, and filemode; each is separated from the previous word by one or more blanks. (The filetype and filemode may be blank if the program is being executed from storage, in which case the SOURCE string will have one or two asterisks as place holders.) Following the filemode is the name by which the program was invoked (which may not be the same as the filename).

The string parsed might therefore look like this:

```
CMS COMMAND REXXTRY XEDIT * rexxt
```

For PARSE VALUE

The *expression* is evaluated, and the resulting character string is parsed. If no expression is given, then the null string is used. Thus, for example:

```
parse value time() with  hours ':' mins ':' secs
```

will get the current time and split it up into its constituent parts.

Note: WITH is a sub-keyword in this context and is reserved because it marks the end of the expression. It cannot be used as a symbol within the expression.

For PARSE VAR name

The value of the variable specified by *name* is parsed. The *name* must be a symbol that is valid as a variable name (*i.e.*, it may not start with a period or a digit).

The variable itself is not changed unless it appears in the template, so that for example:

```
parse var string word1 string
```

will remove the first word from STRING and put it in the variable WORD1, and assign the remainder back to STRING. Similarly

```
parse upper var string word1 string
```

will also translate the data from STRING to upper case before it is parsed.

For PARSE VERSION

Information describing the language level and the date of the language processor is parsed. This consists of five words delimited by blanks.

1. A word describing the language. The first four letters will be the characters "REXX", and the remainder may be used to identify a particular implementation or language processor. This word may not include any periods.

2. The language level description. For example, "4.00". Numbers smaller than this may be assumed to indicate a subset of the language defined here.

3. Three tokens describing the language processor release date in the same format as the default for the DATE() function (see page 92). For example, "16 Oct 1989".

PROCEDURE

PROCEDURE [EXPOSE *variablelist*] ;

where *variablelist* is one or more symbols (optionally enclosed in parentheses) separated by blanks.

The PROCEDURE instruction may be used within an internal routine (subroutine or function) to protect all the existing variables by making them unknown to following instructions. Selected variables may be exposed to the internal routine by using the EXPOSE option. On executing a RETURN instruction, the original variables environment is restored, and any variables used in the routine which were not exposed are dropped.

A routine need not include a PROCEDURE instruction, in which case the variables it is manipulating are those "owned" by the caller. If a PROCEDURE instruction is included, it must be the first instruction executed after the CALL or function invocation – that is, it must be the first instruction following the label.

If the EXPOSE option is used, then the specified variables of the caller are exposed, so that any references to them (including setting them and dropping them) refer to the variables environment owned by the caller. Hence the values of existing variables are accessible, and any changes are persistent even on RETURN from the routine.

The symbols in *variablelist* must be valid variable names and are exposed in sequence from left to right. If the variable name is enclosed in parentheses (blanks are not necessary either inside or outside the parentheses, but may be added if desired) then it is a *variable reference*. The variable itself is exposed and then its value is immediately used as a subsidiary variable list which must follow the same rules as the original list except that no parentheses are allowed.[30] There must be only one variable name between the parentheses in each variable reference, though there may be more than one variable reference in *variablelist*. The variables named in subsidiary lists are also exposed in sequence from left to right.

It is not an error to specify a name more than once, or to specify a name that has not been used as a variable by the caller.

---

[30] That is, it is a list of symbols that must be valid variable names, separated by blanks. Leading and trailing blanks are allowed.

Example:

```
/* This is the main program */
j=1; x.1='a'
call somevars
say j k m        /* would display "1 7 M" */
exit

/* This is a subroutine */
Somevars: procedure expose j k x.j
   say j k x.j /* would display "1 K a"   */
   k=7; m=3     /* note "M" is not exposed */
   return
```

Note that if the "X.J" in the EXPOSE list had been placed before the "J", then the caller's value of "J" would not have been visible at that time, so "X.1" would not have been exposed.

Subsidiary lists can be used simply to make it easier to expose a number of variables at once, or (in conjunction with the VALUE built-in function – see page 112) can be used to allow the manipulation of dynamically named variables.

Example:

```
/* This is the main program */
a=11; b=12; c=13
showlist='a b'  /* but not C */
call playvars
say a b c d      /* would display "11 New 13 9" */
exit

/* This is a subroutine */
Playvars: procedure expose (showlist) d
   say word(showlist,2)            /* would display "b" */
   /* next line would display "12" and set new value */
   say value(word(showlist,2),'New')
   /* next line would display "New" */
   say value(word(showlist,2))
   c=8  /* "C" is not exposed          */
   d=9  /* "D" was exposed explicitly */
   return
```

An entire collection of compound variables (see page 33) may be exposed by specifying their stem in the variable list (or in a subsidiary list). Again, the variables are exposed for all operations.

Example:

```
procedure expose j k a. b.
/* This exposes "J", "K", and all variables whose */
/* name starts with "A." or "B."                  */
a.1='7'  /* This will set "A.1" in the caller's   */
         /* environment, even if it did not       */
         /* previously exist.                     */
```

Notes:

1. Variables may be exposed through several generations of routines, if
    desired, by ensuring that they are included (exposed) on all intermediate
    PROCEDURE instructions.

2. See the CALL instruction and Function descriptions on pages 43 and
    77 for details and examples of how routines are invoked.

PULL

PULL [*template*] ;

where *template* is a list of symbols separated by blanks and/or patterns.

PULL is used to read a string from the external data queue. (See page 139
for a discussion of the REXX input/output model.) It is just a shorter form
of the instruction

```
PARSE UPPER PULL [template];
```

The current head-of-queue will be read as one string. If no template is specified, no further action is taken (and the string is thus effectively discarded).
Otherwise, the string is translated to upper case and then parsed into variables according to the rules described in the section on parsing (page 118).
Use the PARSE PULL instruction if upper case translation is not desired.

Example:

```
say 'Do you want to erase the file?  Answer Yes or No:'
pull answer .
if answer='YES' then Erase oldfile
```

Here the dummy placeholder "." is used on the template so the first word
entered by the user is isolated, ready for the comparison. Since the word
assigned to ANSWER was translated to upper case, the comparison is robust
even though the original response may have been entered in mixed case.

If the external data queue is empty, a line will be read from the default character input stream, and the program will pause if necessary until a line is complete.[31]

The number of lines currently in the external data queue may be found with the QUEUED built-in function, described on page 103.

PUSH

```
    PUSH  [expression];
```

The string resulting from the evaluation of the expression will be stacked LIFO (Last In, First Out) onto the external data queue. (See page 139 for a discussion of the REXX input/output model.) If no expression is specified, a null string is stacked.

Example:

```
a='Soup'
push           /* Puts a null line onto the queue   */
push a 4 2     /* Puts "Soup 4 2"    onto the queue */
```

The number of lines currently in the external data queue may be found with the QUEUED built-in function, described on page 103.

---

[31] That is, as though PARSE UPPER LINEIN had been executed instead (see page 62).

QUEUE

```
QUEUE [expression];
```

The string resulting from the evaluation of the expression will be queued onto the external data queue ("stacked" FIFO – First In, First Out). If no expression is specified, a null string is queued. See page 139 for a discussion of the REXX input/output model.

Example:

```
a='Send me'
queue a 2  /* Enqueues "Send me 2" */
queue      /* Enqueues a null line behind the last */
```

The number of lines currently in the external data queue may be found with the QUEUED built-in function, described on page 103.

RETURN

```
RETURN [expression];
```

RETURN is used to return control (and possibly a result) from a REXX program or internal routine to the point of its invocation.

If no internal routine (subroutine or function) is active, then RETURN has the identical effect on the program that is being executed as EXIT (see page 54).

If a **subroutine** is being executed (see the CALL instruction, on page 43) then the expression (if any) is evaluated, active control constructs are terminated, control passes back to the caller, and the special variable RESULT is set to the value of the expression. If no expression was specified, the variable RESULT is dropped (becomes uninitialized). The various settings saved at the time of the CALL (tracing, addresses, *etc.*) are restored.

If a **function** is being executed, then the action taken is the same, except that an expression **must** be specified on the RETURN instruction. The result of the expression is then used in the original expression at the point where the function was invoked. See the description of functions on page 77 for more details.

Note: If a PROCEDURE instruction was executed within the routine (subroutine or internal function), then all local variables are dropped (and the previous generation is exposed) after the expression is evaluated and before the result is used or assigned to the special variable RESULT.

SAY

SAY [*expression*] ;

SAY writes a line to to the default output character stream. This typically causes it to be displayed (or spoken, or typed, *etc.*) to the user.

Example:

```
data=100
say data 'divided by 4 =>' data/4
/* would display:  "100 divided by 4 => 25"  */
```

The result of evaluating the *expression* is written from the program via the default character output stream, using the appropriate implementation-dependent mechanism for terminating lines. See page 139 for a discussion of the REXX input/output model. The result of the expression may be of any length, and if no expression is specified, the null string is written.

The SAY instruction is a shorter form of the instruction

```
CALL LINEOUT ,[expression];
```

except that SAY does not affect the special variable RESULT. See page 100 for details of the LINEOUT function.

SELECT

SELECT ;   *whenlist* [OTHERWISE [;] [*instructionlist*]]   END ;

where *whenlist* is:

    one or more *whenconstruct*s

and *whenconstruct* is:

    WHEN *expression* [;] THEN [;] *instruction*

and *instructionlist* is:

    any sequence of *instructions*

SELECT is used to conditionally execute one of several alternative instructions.

Each expression following a WHEN is evaluated in turn and must result in '0' or '1'. If the result is '1', then the instruction following the associated THEN (which may be a complex instruction such as IF, DO, or SELECT) is executed and control will then pass directly to the END. If the result is '0', control will pass to the next WHEN clause.

If none of the WHEN expressions result in '1', then control will pass to the instruction list (if any) following OTHERWISE. In this situation, the absence of an OTHERWISE is an error (but note that the instruction list that follows may still be omitted).

Example:

```
Testfile myfile
select
  when rc=0 then do
    Erase myfile
    say 'File' myfile 'existed, now erased'
    end
  when rc=28 | rc=36 then say myfile 'does not exist'
  otherwise
    say 'Unexpected return code "'rc'" from TESTFILE'
    exit rc
end /* Select */
```

Notes:

1.   An *instruction* may be any assignment, command, or keyword instruction, including any of the more complex constructions such as DO and IF and the SELECT instruction itself. A null clause is not an instruction, however, so putting an extra semicolon (or label) after a THEN clause is not equivalent to putting a dummy instruction (as it would be in PL/I). The NOP instruction is provided for this purpose.

2. The keyword THEN is treated specially, in that it need not start a
    clause. This allows the expression on the WHEN clause to be termi-
    nated by the THEN, without a ";" being required – this is consistent
    with the treatment of THEN following an IF clause. Hence the symbol
    THEN cannot be used within the expression.

SIGNAL

$$\text{SIGNAL} \begin{cases} labelname \\ [\text{VALUE}] \; expression \\ \text{ON } condition \; [\text{NAME } trapname] \\ \text{OFF } condition \end{cases} ;$$

where *labelname* is a symbol or literal string which is taken as a constant, and *condition* and *trapname* are single symbols which are taken
as constants.

The SIGNAL instruction causes an **abnormal** change in the flow of control,
or (if ON or OFF is specified) controls the trapping of certain conditions (see
page 145).

If neither ON nor OFF is specified, a label name is derived directly from
labelname. This must be a symbol, which is treated literally, or a literal
string. Alternatively, the label name is taken from the result of evaluating
the expression following VALUE. The sub-keyword VALUE may be omitted
if the expression does not begin with a symbol or a literal string (*i.e.*, if it
starts with a special character, such as an operator character or parenthesis).

All active pending DO loops, DO groups, IF constructs, SELECT constructs,
and INTERPRET instructions in the current routine are then terminated
(*i.e.*, they cannot be reactivated). Control then passes to the first label in the
program that matches the given name, as though the search had started from
the top of the program. If *labelname* is a symbol, the matching takes place
independently of alphabetic case, but otherwise the label must match exactly.

Example:

```
signal bill;  /* Jump to label BILL below */
   ....
   ....
Bill: say 'Hi!'
```

When control reaches the specified label, the line number of the SIGNAL
instruction is assigned to the special variable SIGL. This can be used as an
aid to debugging, as it may be used to determine the source of a jump to a
label.

Using SIGNAL VALUE

The VALUE form of the SIGNAL instruction allows a branch to a label whose name is determined at the time of execution. This can safely be used to effect a form of multi-way CALL (or function call) to internal routines, because any DO loops, *etc.*, in the calling routine are protected against termination by the call mechanism.

Example:

```
fred='pete'
call multiway fred, 7
  ....
  ....
Multiway: procedure
  arg label .         /* One word, upper case */
  /* Could add checks for valid labels here */
  signal value label    /* Jump to wherever */
  ....
Pete: say arg(1) '!' arg(2)
  /* Would display:  pete ! 7 */
  return
```

TRACE

$$\text{TRACE} \begin{bmatrix} \textit{tracesetting} \\ [\text{VALUE}] \ \textit{expression} \end{bmatrix};$$

where *tracesetting* is a symbol or literal string which is taken as a constant.

The TRACE instruction is used to control the tracing of execution of a REXX program, and is primarily used for debugging. Its syntax is more concise than other REXX instructions, since it is commonly entered manually during interactive tracing. For this use economy of keystrokes is considered to be more important than readability.

The trace setting is either taken directly from *tracesetting*, or is taken from the result of evaluating the expression following VALUE. The sub-keyword VALUE may be omitted if the expression does not begin with a symbol or a literal string (*i.e.*, if it starts with a special character, such as an operator character or parenthesis).

The setting may be a whole number. If this is positive, then (if tracing interactively) that number of interactive pauses are skipped (see the section on interactive tracing, page 151, for further information). If the setting is a negative whole number, then all tracing (including interactive pauses) is temporarily inhibited for that number of clauses that would otherwise be traced. For example, "TRACE -100" means that the next 100 clauses that would normally be traced will not in fact be displayed, but then tracing will resume as before.

If the setting is not a whole number, then it may start with one or more "?" characters. If so, these will either switch on or switch off interactive tracing (see below). If any other characters are in the setting then TRACE will take action according to the first of them.

Example:

```
trace ?r
/* Results of expressions will now be traced, and */
/* interactive tracing is switched on if it was   */
/* off before (or vice versa).                    */
```

The permitted values for the alphabetic part of the setting are:

A (e.g., "All") all clauses are traced before execution.

C (e.g., "Commands") all commands are traced before execution. If the command results in an error or failure, then the return code from the command is also shown.

E (e.g., "Error") any command resulting in an error or failure is traced (after execution) together with the return code from the command.

F (e.g., "Failure") any command resulting in a failure is traced (after execution) together with the return code from the command. This is the same as the default setting, "TRACE N".

I (e.g., "Intermediates") as "R" except that all terms and intermediate results during expression evaluation (and substituted names) are also traced.

L (e.g., "Labels") only traces labels passed during execution. This is especially useful while tracing interactively, when the language processor will pause after each label; or if one wishes to note all internal subroutine calls and jumps due to the SIGNAL instruction.

N (e.g., "Normal") nothing is traced except for commands resulting in failure. These are traced (after execution) together with the return code from the command. **This is the default setting.**

O (e.g., "Off") nothing is traced, and interactive tracing is also switched off.

R (e.g., "Results") all clauses are traced before execution, together with the final result of any expression evaluated. Values assigned during PULL, ARG, and PARSE instructions are also displayed. **This setting is recommended for general debugging.**

If no setting is specified, or if the setting is the null string, then tracing is reset to its initial (default) setting, that is, "Normal" tracing with "Interactive tracing OFF".

The current trace setting may be retrieved by using the TRACE built-in function. See page 110.

If available at the time of execution, comments included in a traced clause appear in the trace, as do comments in a null clause if TRACE "A", "I", or "R" is specified.

For "TRACE A" and for "TRACE C", commands traced before execution have the final value of the command (that is, the string passed to the environment) traced as well as the clause generating it. Whenever any command which results in an error or failure is traced the return code from the command is also traced.

Note: The trace setting is automatically saved across internal subroutine and function calls. See the CALL instruction (page 43) for more details.

Interactive trace setting

The "?" prefix on the trace setting is used to control interactive tracing. During normal execution, executing a TRACE instruction with a "?" setting prefix causes interactive tracing to be switched on (see separate section on page 151 for details). While tracing interactively, interpretation will pause after most clauses that are traced; and TRACE instructions in the program are ignored (this is so you are not taken out of interactive tracing unexpectedly). The state of interactive tracing (*i.e.*, whether it is on or off) is saved and restored across internal routine calls.

As an example, the instruction: "TRACE ?Errors" will make the language processor pause for input after executing any command that returns a non-zero return code.

Interactive tracing may be switched off by executing a TRACE instruction with a prefix "?" during an interactive pause, or by executing "TRACE Off". Using the "?" prefix therefore switches you alternately in or out of interactive tracing. The prefix may be specified more than once in the same setting, if desired, and each occurrence of the prefix reverses the previous setting.

The format of TRACE output

Every clause traced will be displayed with automatic formatting (indentation) according to its logical depth of nesting *etc.*, and any control codes in the encoding of the data (for example, EBCDIC values less than '40'x, or ASCII values less than '20'x) may be replaced by a question mark ("?") to avoid console interference. Results (if requested) are indented an extra two spaces and have a double quote prefixed and suffixed so that leading and trailing blanks are apparent. The first clause traced on any line will be preceded by its line number.

All lines displayed during tracing have a three character prefix to identify the type of data being traced. These may be:

-   identifies the source of a single clause, *i.e.*, the data actually in the program.

+++   identifies a trace message. This may be an error or failure return code from a command (for example, +++ RC=27 +++), a prompt message when interactive tracing starts, an indication of a syntax error when tracing interactively, or the traceback clauses after a syntax error in the program (see below).

>>>   identifies the result of an expression (for TRACE Results), or the value assigned to a variable during parsing, or the value returned from a call to a subroutine or function.

>.>   identifies the value "assigned" to a placeholder during parsing (see page 122).

The following prefixes are only used if "TRACE Intermediates" is in effect:

>V>   The string traced is the contents of a variable.

>L>   The string traced is literal (constant symbol, uninitialized variable, or literal string).

>F>   The string traced is the result of a function call.

>P>   The string traced is the result of a prefix operation.

>O>   The string traced is the result of an operation on two terms.

>C>   The string traced is the name of a compound variable. It is traced after substitution and before use, provided that the name had the value of another variable substituted into it.

Please see page 56 for an example of trace output.

If a syntax error occurs and it is not trapped by SIGNAL ON SYNTAX, then the clause in error will be traced, as will any CALL or INTERPRET instructions or clauses with function invocations active at the time of the error. If the error was caused by an attempted jump to a label that could not be found, that label is also included in the traceback. These traceback lines are identified by the special trace prefix "+++".

Notes:

1.   When a loop is being traced, the DO clause itself will be traced on every iteration of the loop.

2.   With some implementations it may be possible to switch tracing on externally, without requiring modification to the program.

SECTION 8:   FUNCTION CALLS

Calls to internal and external routines that return a single result string (called *functions*) may be included in an expression anywhere that a term (such as a literal string) would be valid, using the notation:

---

functionname ([*expression*] [, [*expression*]] ...)

where *functionname* is a symbol or literal string which is taken as a constant.

The expressions (separated by commas) between the parentheses are called the *arguments* to the function. Each argument expression may include further function calls.

It is important to note that the name of the function, *functionname*, must be followed immediately by the "(", with **no** blank in between, or the construct will not be recognized as a function call. (A *blank operator* would be assumed at that point instead.) Only a comment (which has no effect) can appear between the name and the left parenthesis.

The argument expressions are evaluated in turn from left to right and the resulting strings are then passed to the function. This then executes some algorithm (usually dependent on any argument strings passed, though arguments are not mandatory) and will eventually return a single character string. This string is then included in the original expression just as though the entire function reference had been replaced by the name of a variable which contained that returned data.

For example, the function SUBSTR is built-in to the REXX language (see below, page 107) and could be used as:

```
c='abcdefghijk'
a='Part of C is:' Substr(c,3,7)
/* would set A to "Part of C is: cdefghi" */
```

A function may have a variable number of arguments: only those required need be specified. For example, `Substr('ABCDEF',4)` would return `'DEF'`.

The function calling mechanism is identical to that for subroutines, and indeed the only difference in execution between functions and subroutines is that functions must return data, whereas subroutines need not. The various types of routines that can be called as functions may be:

Internal If the routine name exists as a label in the program, then the current state of interpretation is saved, so that it will later be possible to return to the point of invocation to resume execution. Control is then passed to the first label in the program that matches the name.

As with routines invoked by the CALL instructions, certain other state information (TRACE and NUMERIC settings, *etc.*) is saved too. Please see the CALL instruction (page 43) for details. A multi-way function call to internal routines can be effected with the aid of the SIGNAL instruction (see page 73).

If an internal routine is to be called as a function, then any RETURN instruction executed to return from it *must* have an expression specified. This is not necessary if it is only called as a subroutine.

Built-in A rich set of functions are "built-in" as part of the REXX language: these are always available, and are defined in the next section (pages 81-117).

External It is usually possible to write or make use of functions that are external to a program. These external routines may be written in any language (including REXX) which supports the implementation-dependent interfaces used by REXX to invoke it. A REXX program may be invoked as a function, and in this case may be passed more than one argument string. These may be retrieved by using the ARG or PARSE ARG instructions, or the ARG built-in function. Since the program is called as a function it must return data to the caller.

Calling an external REXX program as a function is similar to calling an internal routine. The external routine is however an implicit PROCEDURE in that all the caller's variables are always hidden, and the state of internal values (NUMERIC settings, *etc.*) starts with their defaults (rather than inheriting those of the caller). In addition, EXIT may be used to return from the routine.

Here is an example of a call to an **internal** function.

Example:

FACTOR2

```
/* Recursive internal function execution... */
arg x
say x'! =' factorial(x)
exit

Factorial: procedure    /* calculate factorial by.. */
   arg n                /* .. recursive invocation. */
   if n=0 then return 1
   return factorial(n-1)*n
```

FACTORIAL is unusual in that it invokes itself (this is known as "recursive invocation"). The PROCEDURE instruction ensures that a new variable N is created for each call. (This example may be compared with the example on page 45 in which CALL is used to invoke a similar factorial routine.)

If an external or built-in function detects an error of any kind, then REXX is informed, and a syntax error is raised. Execution of the clause that included the function call is therefore terminated. Similarly, if an external function fails to return data correctly, this will be detected by the language processor and reported as an error.

If a syntax error occurs during the execution of an internal function, it may be trapped (using SIGNAL ON SYNTAX) and recovery may then be possible. If the error is not trapped, then execution of the whole program is terminated in the usual way.

Implementation minimum: As for the CALL instruction, at least 10 argument expressions should be allowed in a function call.

The search order for functions

REXX searches for functions in the order given above – that is, internal labels take precedence, then built-in functions, and finally external functions (the last may have their own search order, but this is an implementation-dependent matter). However, internal labels are **not** used if the function name is given as a literal string (*i.e.*, is specified in quotes) – in this case the function must be built-in or external. This lets you usurp the name of (say) a built-in function to extend its capabilities, yet still be able to invoke the built-in function when needed.

Example:

```
/* Modified DATE to return standard date by default */
Date: procedure
      arg in
      if in='' then in='Standard'
      return 'DATE'(in)
```

Note that the built-in functions have upper case names, and so the name in the literal string must be in upper case for the search to succeed, as in the example. The same is often true of external functions.

Note: Execution of a function with a variable function name may be achieved by careful use of the INTERPRET instruction, however this should be avoided if possible as it reduces the clarity of the program. A better strategy is to pass the varying parameter as an argument to the function, if possible.

SECTION 9:   BUILT-IN FUNCTIONS

There is a rich set of built-in functions defined as part of the REXX language. These include character manipulation, conversion, and information functions. Further external functions are generally available, as appropriate for the system under which the REXX language processor runs.

General notes on the built-in functions:

- The parentheses in a function call are always needed, even if no arguments are required. The first parenthesis must immediately follow the name of the function, with no space in between.

- The arguments named as a *number* are rounded, if necessary, according to the current setting of NUMERIC DIGITS (just as though the number had been added to 0), and checked for validity before use.[32] Except for these uses, the built-in functions work internally with NUMERIC DIGITS 9 and NUMERIC FUZZ 0 and are unaffected by changes to the NUMERIC settings.

- Any argument named as a *string* may be a null string.

- If an argument specifies a length, then it must be a non-negative whole number. If it specifies a start character or word in a string, then it must be a positive whole number unless otherwise stated.

- Where the last argument is optional, a comma may always be included to indicate that it has been omitted. For example, DATATYPE(1,) would return 'NUM'.

- A *pad* argument, if specified, must be exactly one character long.

- If a function has a sub-option selected by the first character of a string, that character may be in upper or lower case.

- Conversion between characters and hexadecimal is dependent on the machine representation (encoding) of character strings, and hence will return appropriately different results for ASCII, EBCDIC, and other encodings. The examples below use an EBCDIC encoding.

---

[32] These are used in the mathematical functions ABS, FORMAT, MAX, MIN, SIGN, and TRUNC, and also apply to certain options of the DATATYPE function.

ABBREV(information,info[,length])

returns 1 if *info* is equal to the leading characters of *information* **and** *info* is not less than the minimum length, *length*. Returns 0 if either of these conditions is not met. The minimum length may be specified as the third argument; the default is the length of *info*.

Examples:

```
ABBREV('Print','Pri')    == 1
ABBREV('PRINT','Pri')    == 0
ABBREV('PRINT','PRI',4)  == 0
ABBREV('PRINT','PRY')    == 0
ABBREV('PRINT','')       == 1
ABBREV('PRINT','',1)     == 0
```

Note: A null string will always match if a length of 0 (or the default) is used. This allows a default keyword to be selected automatically if desired.

Example:

```
say 'Enter option:';   pull option .
select  /* keyword1 is to be the default */
  when abbrev('keyword1',option) then ...
  when abbrev('keyword2',option) then ...
     ...
  otherwise ...
  end
```

ABS(number)

returns the absolute value of *number*. The result has no sign and is formatted according to the current NUMERIC settings.

Examples:

```
ABS('12.3')     == 12.3
ABS(' -0.307') == 0.307
```

ADDRESS()

returns the name of the environment to which commands are currently being submitted. See the ADDRESS instruction (page 40) for more information.

Examples:

```
ADDRESS() == 'PCDOS'  /* perhaps */
ADDRESS() == 'XEDIT'  /* perhaps */
```

ARG([n[,option]])

returns an argument string, or information about the argument strings to a program or internal routine.

If n is not specified, the number of arguments passed to the program or internal routine is returned (see note below).

If only n is specified, the nth argument string is returned. If the argument string does not exist, the null string is returned. n must be a positive whole number.

If *option* is specified, the function tests for the existence of the nth argument string. Possible values for *option* (of which only the first character is significant) are:

E   (Exists); returns 1 if the nth argument exists; that is, if it was explicitly specified as an argument string when the routine was invoked. Returns 0 otherwise.

O   (Omitted); returns 1 if the nth argument was omitted; that is, if it was **not** explicitly specified when the routine was invoked. Returns 0 otherwise.

Examples:

```
/* Following "Call name;" (no arguments) */
ARG()          ==  0
ARG(1)         ==  ''
ARG(2)         ==  ''
ARG(1,'e')  ==  0
ARG(1,'O')  ==  1

/* Following "Call name 1,,2;" */
ARG()          ==  3
ARG(1)         ==  1
ARG(2)         ==  ''
ARG(3)         ==  2
ARG(n)         ==  ''        /* for n>=4 */
ARG(1,'e')  ==  1
ARG(2,'E')  ==  0
ARG(2,'O')  ==  1
ARC(3,'o')  ==  0
ARG(4,'o')  ==  1
```

Notes:

1.   The number of argument strings is the largest number n for which ARG(n,'e') would return 1. That is, the position of the last explicitly specified string.

2.   The argument strings to a program may be retrieved and parsed directly using the ARG or PARSE ARG instructions – see pages 42 and 62.

3.   Programs called as commands can only have 0 or 1 argument strings.

BITAND(string1[,[string2][,pad]])

returns a string composed of the two input strings logically ANDed together, bit by bit. (That is, it is the encodings of the strings that are used in the logical operation.)

The length of the result is the length of the longer of the two strings. If no *pad* character is provided, then the AND operation terminates when the shorter of the two strings is exhausted and the unprocessed portion of the longer string is appended to the partial result. If *pad* is provided, it is used to extend the shorter of the two strings on the right, before carrying out the logical operation. The default for *string2* is the zero length (null) string.

Examples:

```
BITAND('73'x,'27'x)            ==  '23'x
BITAND('13'x,'5555'x)          ==  '1155'x
BITAND('13'x,'5555'x,'74'X) ==  '1154'x
```

BITOR(string1[,[string2][,pad]])

returns a string composed of the two input strings logically (inclusively) ORed together, bit by bit. (That is, it is the encodings of the strings that are used in the logical operation.)

The length of the result is the length of the longer of the two strings. If no *pad* character is provided, then the OR operation terminates when the shorter of the two strings is exhausted and the unprocessed portion of the longer string is appended to the partial result. If *pad* is provided, it is used to extend the shorter of the two strings on the right, before carrying out the logical operation. The default for *string2* is the zero length (null) string.

Examples:

```
BITOR('15'x,'24'x)            ==  '35'x
BITOR('15'x,'2456'x)          ==  '3556'x
BITOR('15'x,'2456'x,'F0'x) ==  '35F6'x
BITOR('1111'x,,'4D'x)         ==  '5D5D'x
```

BITXOR(string1[,[string2][,pad]])

returns a string composed of the two input strings logically eXclusive ORed together, bit by bit. (That is, it is the encodings of the strings that are used in the logical operation.)

The length of the result is the length of the longer of the two strings. If no *pad* character is provided, then the XOR operation terminates when the shorter of the two strings is exhausted and the unprocessed portion of the longer string is appended to the partial result. If *pad* is provided, it is used to extend the shorter of the two strings on the right, before carrying out the logical operation. The default for *string2* is the zero length (null) string.

Examples:

```
BITXOR('12'x,'22'x)             == '30'x
BITXOR('1211'x,'22'x)           == '3011'x
BITXOR('C711'x,'222222'x,' ')   == 'E53362'x
BITXOR('1111'x,'444444'x)       == '555544'x
BITXOR('1111'x,'444444'x,'40'x) == '555504'x
BITXOR('1111'x,,'4D'x)          == '5C5C'x
```

B2X(binary-string)

Binary to Hexadecimal. Converts *binary-string*, a string of binary (0 and/or 1) digits, to an equivalent string of hexadecimal characters. The returned string will use upper case alphabetics for the values A-F, and will not include any blanks.

binary-string may be of any length, and if it is the null string then a null string is returned. If the number of binary digits in the string is not a multiple of four, then up to three '0' digits will be added on the left before conversion to make a total that is a multiple of four.

Blanks may optionally be included in *binary-string* (at four-digit boundaries only, corresponding to the returned hexadecimal character boundaries, and not leading or trailing) to aid readability; they are ignored.

Examples:

```
B2X('11000011')      == 'C3'
B2X('10111')         == '17'
B2X('101')           == '5'
B2X('1 1111  0000')  == '1F0'
```

B2X may be combined with the X2D or X2C functions to convert binary strings into other forms.

Example:

```
X2D(B2X('10111'))    == '23'
```

CENTRE(string,length[,pad])

or

CENTER(string,length[,pad])

returns a string of length *length* with *string* centered in it, with *pad* characters added as necessary to make up the required length. *length* must be zero or positive. The default *pad* character is blank. If the string is longer than *length*, it will be truncated at both ends to fit. If an odd number of characters are truncated or added, the right hand end loses or gains one more character than the left hand end.

Examples:

```
CENTRE(abc,7)             == '  ABC  '
CENTRE(abc,8,'-')         == '--ABC---'
CENTER('The blue sky',8)  == 'e blue s'
CENTER('The blue sky',7)  == 'e blue '
```

Note: This function may be called either CENTRE or CENTER, which avoids errors due to the difference between the British and American spellings.

CHARIN([name][,[start][,length]])

returns a string of up to *length* characters read from the character input stream *name*. (See page 139 for a discussion of the REXX input/output model.) The form of the *name* is implementation-dependent. If *name* is omitted, then characters will be read from the default input stream. The default *length* is 1.

For persistent streams, a read position is maintained for each stream. Any read from the stream will by default start at the current read position. When the read is completed the read position is increased by the number of characters read. A *start* value may be given to specify an explicit read position. This read position must be positive and within the bounds of the stream, and must not be specified for a transient stream. A value of 1 for *start* refers to the first character in the stream.

If a *length* of 0 is given, then the read position will be set to the value of *start* but no characters will be read and the null string is returned.

If there are fewer than *length* characters available, then execution of the program will normally stop until sufficient characters do become available. If, however, it is impossible for those characters to become available due to an error or other problem then the NOTREADY condition is raised (see page 142) and CHARIN will return with fewer than the requested number of characters.

Examples:

```
CHARIN(mine,1,3)  ==  'MFC'      /* perhaps */
CHARIN(mine,1,0)  ==  ''         /* now at start */
CHARIN(mine)      ==  'M'        /* after last */
CHARIN(mine,,2)   ==  'FC'       /* after last */
CHARIN()          ==  'a'        /* perhaps */
CHARIN(,,5)       ==  'abc d'    /* perhaps */
```

CHAROUT([name][,[string][,start]])

returns the count of characters remaining after attempting to write *string* to the character output stream *name*. (See page 139 for a discussion of the REXX input/output model.) The form of the *name* is implementation-dependent. If *name* is omitted, then the characters in *string* will be written to the default output stream. *string* may be the null string, in which case no characters are written to the stream and 0 is always returned.

For persistent streams, a write position is maintained for each stream. Any write to the stream will by default start at the current write position. When the write is completed the write position is increased by the number of characters written. The initial write position is the end of the stream, so that calls to CHAROUT will normally append to the end of the stream.

A *start* value may be given to specify an explicit write position for a persistent stream. This write position must be positive and within the bounds of the stream (though it may specify the character position immediately after the end of the stream). A value of 1 for *start* refers to the first character in the stream.[33]

The *string* may be omitted for persistent streams. In this case the write position will be set to the value of *start* that was given, no characters are written to the stream, and 0 is returned. If neither *start* nor *string* are given, then the write position will be set to the end of the stream. This use of CHAROUT may also have the side-effect of closing or fixing the file in environments which support this concept. Again, 0 is returned.

Execution of the program will normally stop until the output operation is effectively complete. If, however, it is impossible for all the characters to be written, then the NOTREADY condition is raised (see page 142) and CHAROUT will return with the number of characters that could not be written (the residual count).

---

[33] In some environments overwriting a stream with CHAROUT or LINEOUT may erase (destroy) all existing data in the stream.

Examples:

```
CHAROUT(mine,'Hi')      ==  0   /* normally */
CHAROUT(mine,'Hi',5)    ==  0   /* normally */
CHAROUT(mine,,6)        ==  0   /* now at char 6 */
CHAROUT(mine)           ==  0   /* end of stream */
CHAROUT(,'Hi')          ==  0   /* normally */
CHAROUT(,'Hello')       ==  2   /* maybe */
```

Note: This routine is often best called as a subroutine. The residual count is then available in the variable RESULT.

Examples:

```
Call CHAROUT myfile,'Hello'
Call CHAROUT myfile,'Hi',6
Call CHAROUT myfile
```

CHARS([name])

returns the total number of characters remaining in the character input stream *name*. The count includes any line separator characters, if these are defined for the stream, and in the case of persistent streams is the count of characters from the current read position. (See page 139 for a discussion of the REXX input/output model.)

The form of the *name* is implementation-dependent. If *name* is omitted, then the number of characters available in the default input stream is returned.

If an implementation cannot determine the count accurately or efficiently, then it may return 1 for any non-zero count or when the count is unknown. An actual character count may therefore be used only in programs specific to a particular environment in which CHARS is fully supported for the specified stream.

Examples:

```
CHARS(myfile)   ==  42   /* perhaps */
CHARS(nonfile)  ==  0    /* perhaps */
CHARS()         ==  27   /* perhaps */
```

Note: The LINES function may be used to return the number of complete lines (rather than individual characters) remaining in the stream.

COMPARE(string1,string2[,pad])

returns 0 if *string1* and *string2* are the same. If they are not, the returned number is positive and is the position of the first character that is not the same in both strings. If one string is shorter than the other, one or more *pad* characters are added on the right to make it the same length for the comparison. The default *pad* character is a blank.

Examples:

```
COMPARE('abc','abc')      == 0
COMPARE('abc','ak')       == 2
COMPARE('ab ','ab')       == 0
COMPARE('ab ','ab',' ')   == 0
COMPARE('ab ','ab','x')   == 3
COMPARE('ab-- ','ab','-') == 5
```

CONDITION([option])

returns the condition information associated with the current trapped condition. (See page 145 for a description of condition traps.) Four pieces of information may be requested: the name of the current trapped condition, any descriptive string associated with that condition, whether the trap caused a SIGNAL or a CALL, and the state of the trapped condition (if any). The following *option* strings (of which only the first letter is needed) may be supplied to select the information returned:

C   (Condition name); returns the name of the current trapped condition.

D   (Description); returns any descriptive string associated with the current trapped condition. The possible strings are listed on page 149. If no description is available, a null string is returned.

I   (Instruction); returns the keyword for the instruction executed when the current condition was trapped, being either 'CALL' or 'SIGNAL'. This is the default if no *option* was specified.

S   (State); returns the state of the current trapped condition. This may change during execution, and will be one of: ON (the condition is enabled); OFF (the condition is disabled); or DELAY (any new occurrence of the condition will be delayed or ignored).

If no condition has been trapped (that is, there is no current trapped condition) then the CONDITION function returns a null string in all four cases.

Examples:

```
CONDITION()     == 'CALL'            /* perhaps */
CONDITION('C') == 'FAILURE'
CONDITION('I') == 'CALL'
CONDITION('D') == 'FailureTest'
CONDITION('S') == 'OFF'
```

Note: The condition information returned by the CONDITION built-in function is saved and restored across subroutine calls (including those caused by a CALL ON condition trap). Therefore, once a subroutine invoked due to a CALL ON trap has returned, the current trapped condition will revert to that which was current before the CALL took place (which may be none); the CONDITION built-in function will then return the values it returned before the condition was trapped.

COPIES(string,n)

returns *n* directly concatenated copies of *string*. *n* must be positive or 0.

Examples:

```
COPIES('abc',3) == 'abcabcabc'
COPIES('abc',0) == ''
```

C2D(string[,n])

Character to Decimal. Returns the decimal value of the binary representation (encoding) of *string*. If the result cannot be expressed as a whole number, an error results – that is, the result must not have more digits than the current setting of NUMERIC DIGITS.

string may be the null string, in which case 0 is returned.

If *n* is not specified, *string* is taken to be an unsigned number:

Examples:

```
C2D('09'x)    ==       9
C2D('81'x)    ==     129
C2D('a')      ==     129
C2D('FF81'x)  ==   65409
C2D('')       ==       0
```

If *n* is specified, the string is taken as a signed number expressed in *n* characters. If the most significant (left-most) bit is zero then the number is positive; otherwise it is a negative number in two's complement form. In both cases it is converted to a REXX whole number which may therefore be negative. If *n* is 0, 0 is always returned.

The string is padded on the left with characters of '00'X (note, not "sign-extended") or truncated on the left to length *n* characters, if necessary – that is, as though RIGHT(*string*,*n*,'00'x) had been executed.

Examples:

```
C2D('81'x,1)   ==   -127
C2D('81'x,2)   ==    129
C2D('FF81'x,2) ==   -127
C2D('FF81'x,1) ==   -127
C2D('FF7F'x,1) ==    127
C2D('F081'x,2) ==  -3967
C2D('F081'x,1) ==   -127
C2D('0031'x,0) ==      0
```

C2X(string)

Character to Hexadecimal. Converts the encoding of a character string to its hexadecimal representation (unpacks). The returned string will use upper case alphabetics for the values A-F, and will not include any blanks. The string to be unpacked may be of any length, and if it is the null string then a null string is returned.

Examples:

```
C2X('72s')    ==  'F7F2A2'
C2X('0123'x)  ==  '0123'
```

DATATYPE(string[,type])

If only *string* is specified, the returned result is 'NUM' if *string* is a syntactically valid REXX number that can be added to '0' without error, or 'CHAR' otherwise.

If *type* is specified, the returned result is 1. if *string* matches the type, or 0 otherwise. If *string* is null, 0 is returned (except when *type* is "X", which returns 1 for a null string). The valid *types* (of which only the one letter is needed) are:

A   (Alphanumeric); returns 1 if *string* only contains characters from the ranges "a-z", "A-Z", and "0-9".

B   (Binary); returns 1 if *string* only contains the characters "0" and/or "1".

L   (Lower case); returns 1 if *string* only contains characters from the range "a-z".

M   (Mixed case); returns 1 if *string* only contains characters from the ranges "a-z" and "A-Z".

N   (Number); returns 1 if DATATYPE(*string*) would return 'NUM'.

S   (Symbol); returns 1 if *string* only contains characters that are valid in REXX symbols (see page 21). Note that lower case alphabetics are permitted.

U   (Upper case); returns 1 if *string* only contains characters from the range "A-Z".

W   (Whole number); returns 1 if *string* is a REXX whole number (see page 137) under the current setting of NUMERIC DIGITS.

X   (heXadecimal); returns 1 if *string* only contains characters from the ranges "a-f", "A-F", "0-9", and blank (so long as blanks only appear between pairs of hexadecimal characters, as usual.) Also returns 1 if *string* is a null string, which is a valid hexadecimal string.

Examples:

```
DATATYPE(' 12 ')         ==  'NUM'
DATATYPE('')             ==  'CHAR'
DATATYPE('123*')         ==  'CHAR'
DATATYPE('12.3','N')     ==  1
DATATYPE('12.3','W')     ==  0
DATATYPE('Fred','M')     ==  1
DATATYPE('','M')         ==  0
DATATYPE('Minx','L')     ==  0
DATATYPE('3d?','s')      ==  1
DATATYPE('BCd3','X')     ==  1
DATATYPE('BC d3','X')    ==  1
```

Note: The DATATYPE function tests the meaning, or type, of characters in a string, independent of the encoding of those characters.

DATE([option])

by default returns the local date in the format 'dd Mmm yyyy' (for example, the value might be '27 Aug 1989'), with no leading zero or blank on the day. The first three characters of the English name of the month are used.

The following *option* strings (of which only the first letter is needed) may be supplied to obtain alternative formats:

B   (Base); returns the number of complete days (that is, not including the current day) since and including the base date, 1 Jan 0001, in the format 'dddddd' (no leading zeros or blanks). This base date is determined by extending the current Gregorian calendar backwards (365 days each year, with an extra day every year that is divisible by 4 except century years that are not divisible by 400).

   Note: The expression DATE('B')//7 returns a number corresponding to the day of the week, with 0 indicating Monday. DATE('B') would have returned 693595 on 1 Jan 1900.

D   (Days); returns the number of days, including the current day, so far in this year in the format 'ddd' (no leading zeros or blanks).

E   (European); returns the date in the format 'dd/mm/yy'.

M   (Month); returns the full English name of the current month, in mixed case (first letter a capital).

N   (Normal); explicitly returns the date in default format, as described above.

O   (Ordered); returns the date in the format 'yy/mm/dd' (suitable for sorting, *etc.*).

S   (Standard); returns date in the format `'yyyymmdd'` (suitable for sorting, *etc.*). Note that this is one of the three forms recommended in the International Standards Organization Recommendation ISO/R 2014-1971 (E). The other two forms recommended in that document can be derived from this form by separating the month from the year and day using either blanks or hyphens, thus: `'1989 08 27'` or `'1989-08-27'`.

U   (USA); returns the date in the format `'mm/dd/yy'`.

W   (Weekday); returns the English name for the day of the week, in mixed case (first letter a capital).

Examples:

```
DATE()      ==  '27 Aug 1989'
DATE('B')   ==  726340
DATE('D')   ==  239
DATE('E')   ==  '27/08/89'
DATE('M')   ==  'August'
DATE('N')   ==  '27 Aug 1989'
DATE('O')   ==  '89/08/27'
DATE('S')   ==  '19890827'
DATE('U')   ==  '08/27/89'
DATE('w')   ==  'Saturday'
```

Note: The first call to DATE or TIME in one clause causes a record of the time to be made which is then used for **all** calls to these functions within that clause. Hence if multiple calls to DATE and/or TIME are made in a single expression or clause, then they are guaranteed to be consistent with each other.

DELSTR(string,n[,length])

deletes the sub-string of *string* that begins at the nth character, and is of length *length*. If *length* is not specified, the rest of the string is deleted (including the nth character). *length* must be non-negative, and n must be positive. If n is greater than the length of *string*, the string is returned unchanged.

Examples:

```
DELSTR('abcd',3)     ==  'ab'
DELSTR('abcde',3,2)  ==  'abe'
DELSTR('abcde',6)    ==  'abcde'
```

DELWORD(string,n[,length])

deletes the sub-string of *string* that starts at the nth word, and is of length *length* blank-delimited words. If *length* is omitted it defaults to be the remaining words in the string (including the nth word). *length* must be non-negative, and *n* must be positive. If *n* is greater than the number of words in *string*, the string is returned unchanged. The string deleted includes any blanks following the final word involved, but none of the blanks preceding the first word involved.

Examples:

```
DELWORD('Now is the  time',2,2) == 'Now time'
DELWORD('Now is the time ',3)   == 'Now is '
DELWORD('Now  time',5)          == 'Now  time'
```

DIGITS()

returns the current setting of NUMERIC DIGITS. See the NUMERIC instruction (page 59) for more information.

Example:

```
DIGITS() == 9   /* if default */
```

D2C(whole-number[,n])

Decimal to Character. Returns a character string of length as needed, or of length *n*, which is the binary representation of the decimal number.

Whole-number must be a non-negative number unless *n* is specified, or an error will result. If *n* is not specified, the length of the result returned is such that there are no leading '00'x characters.

If *n* is specified it is the length of the final result in characters; that is, after conversion the input string will be sign-extended to the required length. If the number is too big to fit into *n* characters, it will be truncated on the left. *n* must be non-negative.

Examples:

```
D2C(9)        == '09'x
D2C(129)      == '81'x
D2C(129,1)    == '81'x
D2C(129,2)    == '0081'x
D2C(257,1)    == '01'x
D2C(-127,1)   == '81'x
D2C(-127,2)   == 'FF81'x
D2C(-1,4)     == 'FFFFFFFF'x
D2C(12,0)     == ''
```

D2X(whole-number[,n])

Decimal to Hexadecimal. Returns a string of hexadecimal characters of length as needed or of length n, which is the hexadecimal (unpacked) representation of the decimal number. The returned string will use upper case alphabetics for the values A-F, and will not include any blanks.

Whole-number must be a non-negative number unless n is specified, or an error will result. If n is not specified, the length of the result returned is such that there are no leading '0' characters.

If n is specified it is the length of the final result in characters; that is, after conversion the input string will be sign-extended to the required length. If the number is too big to fit into n characters, it will be truncated on the left. n must be non-negative.

Examples:

```
D2X(9)        ==  '9'
D2X(129)      ==  '81'
D2X(129,1)    ==  '1'
D2X(129,2)    ==  '81'
D2X(129,4)    ==  '0081'
D2X(257,2)    ==  '01'
D2X(-127,2)   ==  '81'
D2X(-127,4)   ==  'FF81'
D2X(12,0)     ==  ''
```

Note: A call to D2X is similar to a call to D2C followed by a call to C2X, except that an odd number of characters can be returned.

ERRORTEXT(n)

returns the REXX error message associated with error number n. n must be in the range 0-99, and any other value is an error. If n is in the allowed range, but is not a defined REXX error number, the null string is returned. The text will be returned in the language appropriate to the implementation.

Examples:

```
ERRORTEXT(16)  ==  'Label not found'
ERRORTEXT(60)  ==  ''
```

FORM()

> returns the current setting of NUMERIC FORM. See the NUMERIC instruction (page 59) for more information.

> **Example:**

> ```
> FORM() == 'SCIENTIFIC'   /* if default */
> ```

FORMAT(number[,[before][,[after]]])

> rounds and formats *number*.

> The *number* is first rounded according to standard REXX rules, just as though the operation "number+0" had been carried out. If only *number* is given, the result is precisely that of this operation.

> The arguments *before* and *after* may be specified to control the number of characters to be used for the integer part and decimal part of the result respectively. If either of these is omitted the number of characters used will be as many as are needed for that part.

> If *before* is not large enough to contain the integer part of the number, an error results. If *after* is not the same size as the decimal part of the number, the number will be rounded (or extended with zeros) to fit. Specifying 0 will cause the number to be rounded to an integer (that is, it will have no decimal part).

> **Examples:**

> ```
> FORMAT('3',4)            == '   3'
> FORMAT('1.73',4,0)       == '   2'
> FORMAT('1.73',4,3)       == '   1.730'
> FORMAT('-.76',4,1)       == '  -0.8'
> FORMAT('3.03',4)         == '   3.03'
> FORMAT(' - 12.73',,4)    == '-12.7300'
> FORMAT(' - 12.73')       == '-12.73'
> FORMAT('0.000')          == '0'
> ```

> A further two arguments may be passed to the FORMAT function to control the use of exponential notation. The full syntax of the function is therefore:

FORMAT(number[,[before][,[after][,[expp][,expt]]]])

> The first three arguments are as described above, and in addition *expp* and *expt* control the exponent part of the result, which by default is formatted according to the current NUMERIC settings of DIGITS and FORM. *expp* sets the number of places (digits) to be used for the exponent part, the default being to use as many as are needed. *expt* sets the trigger point for use of exponential notation. If the number of places needed for the integer or decimal part exceeds *expt* or twice *expt* respectively, exponential notation will be used. The default is the cur-

rent setting of NUMERIC DIGITS. If 0 is specified for *expt*, exponential notation is always used unless the exponent would be 0.

If 0 is specified for the *expp* field, no exponent will be supplied, and the number will be expressed in "simple" form with added zeros as necessary.[34] Otherwise, if *expp* is not large enough to contain the exponent, an error results. If *expp* is non-zero and the exponent will be 0, then *expp*+2 blanks are supplied for the exponent part of the result.

Examples:

```
FORMAT('12345.73',,,2,2)  ==  '1.234573E+04'
FORMAT('12345.73',,3,,0)  ==  '1.235E+4'
FORMAT('1.234573',,3,,0)  ==  '1.235'
FORMAT('123.45',,3,2,0)   ==  '1.235E+02'
FORMAT('1.2345',,3,2,0)   ==  '1.235    '
FORMAT('12345.73',,,3,6)  ==  '12345.73'
FORMAT('1234567e5',,3,0)  ==  '123456700000.000'
```

Note: If NUMERIC FORM ENGINEERING is in effect, up to 3 digits may be needed for the integer part of the result (*before*).

Implementation minimum: If exponents are supported in an implementation, then they must be supported for exponents whose absolute value is at least as large as the largest number that can be expressed as an exact integer in default precision, *i.e.*, 999999999. Therefore, values for *expp* of up to 9 should also be supported.

FUZZ()

returns the current setting of NUMERIC FUZZ. See the NUMERIC instruction (page 59) for more information.

Example:

```
FUZZ() == 0   /* if default */
```

INSERT(new,target[,[n][,[length][,pad]]])

inserts the string *new*, padded to length *length*, into the string *target* after the nth character. *length* and *n* must be non-negative. If *n* is greater than the length of the target string, padding is added before the *new* string also. The default value for *n* is 0, which means insert before the beginning of the string. The default value for *length* is the length of *new*. The default *pad* character is a blank.

---

[34] This overrides a 0 value of *expt* if necessary.

Examples:

```
INSERT(' ','abcdef',3)         == 'abc def'
INSERT('123','abc',5,6)        == 'abc   123   '
INSERT('123','abc',5,6,'+')    == 'abc++123+++'
INSERT('123','abc')            == '123abc'
INSERT('123','abc',,5,'-')     == '123--abc'
```

LASTPOS(needle,haystack[,start])

returns the position of the last occurrence of one string, *needle*, in another, *haystack*. (See also POS.) If the string *needle* is not found, or is the null string, 0 is returned. By default the search starts at the last character of *haystack* and scans backwards. This may be overridden by specifying *start*, the point at which to start the backwards scan. *start* must be a positive whole number, and defaults to LENGTH(*string*) if larger than that value or if not specified.

Examples:

```
LASTPOS(' ','abc def ghi')    == 8
LASTPOS(' ','abcdefghi')      == 0
LASTPOS(' ','abc def ghi',7)  == 4
```

LEFT(string,length[,pad])

returns a string of length *length* containing the left-most *length* characters of *string*. The string is padded with *pad* characters (or truncated) on the right as needed. The default *pad* character is a blank. *length* must be non-negative. This function is exactly equivalent to SUBSTR(*string*,1,*length* [,*pad*]).

Examples:

```
LEFT('abc d',8)       == 'abc d   '
LEFT('abc d',8,'.')   == 'abc d...'
LEFT('abc  def',7)    == 'abc  de'
```

LENGTH(string)

returns the length of *string*.

Examples:

```
LENGTH('abcdefgh')  == 8
LENGTH('')          == 0
```

LINEIN([name][,[line][,count]])

returns *count* (0 or 1) lines read from the character input stream *name*. (See page 139 for a discussion of the REXX input/output model.) The default *count* is 1. The form of the *name* is implementation-dependent. If *name* is omitted, then the line will be read from the default input stream.

For persistent streams (such as random-access files), a read position is maintained for each stream. Any read from the stream will by default start at the current read position.[35] When the read is completed the read position is increased by the number of characters read. A *line* number may be given to set the read position to the start of a specified line. This line number must be positive and within the bounds of the stream, and must not be specified for a transient stream. A value of 1 for *line* refers to the first line in the stream.

If a *count* of 0 is given, then the read position will be set to the start of the specified *line* but no characters will be read and the null string is returned.

If a complete line is not available in the stream, then execution of the program will normally stop until the line is complete. If, however, it is impossible for a line to be completed due to an error or other problem then the NOTREADY condition is raised (see page 142) and LINEIN will return with whatever characters are available.

Examples:

```
LINEIN(mine)      == 'MFC'    /* perhaps */
LINEIN(mine,5)    == 'Line5'  /* perhaps */
LINEIN(mine,5,0)  == ''
LINEIN(mine)      == 'Line5'  /* after last */
LINEIN()          == 'Hello'  /* perhaps */
```

Note: If the intention is to read complete lines from the default character stream, as in a simple dialogue with a user, then the PULL or PARSE PULL instructions should be used instead for simplicity and for improved programmability. The PARSE LINEIN instruction may also be used in certain cases.

---

[35] Under certain circumstances, therefore, a call to LINEIN will return a partial line if the stream has already been read with the CHARIN function, and part but not all of a line (and its termination, if any) has been read.

LINEOUT([name][,[string][,line]])

returns the count of lines remaining after attempting to write *string* as a line to the character output stream *name*. (See page 139 for a discussion of the REXX input/output model.) The count will be either 0 (meaning the line was successfully written) or 1 (meaning that an error occurred while writing the line). *string* may be the null string, in which case only the action associated with completing a line is taken.

The form of the *name* is implementation-dependent. If *name* is omitted, then the line will be written to the default output stream.

For persistent streams, a write position is maintained for each stream. Any write to the stream will by default start at the current write position.[36] When the write is completed the write position is increased by the number of characters written. The initial write position is the end of the stream, so that calls to LINEOUT will normally append lines to the end of the stream.

A *line* number may be given to set the write position to the start of a particular line in a persistent stream. This line number must be positive and within the bounds of the stream (though it may specify the line number immediately after the end of the stream). A value of 1 for *line* refers to the first line in the stream.[37] The *string* may be omitted for persistent streams. In this case the write position will be set to the start of the *line* that was given, nothing is written to the stream, and 0 is returned. If neither *line* nor *string* are given, then the write position will be set to the end of the stream. This use of LINEOUT may also have the side-effect of closing or fixing the file in environments which support this concept. Again, 0 is returned.

Execution of the program will normally stop until the output operation is effectively complete. If, however, it is impossible for a line to be written, then the NOTREADY condition is raised (see page 142) and LINEOUT will return with a result of 1 (this is the residual count of lines written).

---

[36] Under certain circumstances, therefore, the characters written by a call to LINEOUT may be added to a partial line previously written to the stream with the CHAROUT routine. LINEOUT conceptually terminates a line at the **end** of each call.

[37] In some environments overwriting a stream with LINEOUT or CHAROUT may erase (destroy) all existing data in the stream.

Examples:

```
LINEOUT(mine,'Hi')    == 0  /* normally */
LINEOUT(mine,'Hi',5)  == 0  /* normally */
LINEOUT(mine,,6)      == 0  /* now at line 6 */
LINEOUT(mine)         == 0  /* at end stream */
LINEOUT(,'Hi')        == 0  /* normally */
LINEOUT(,'Hello')     == 1  /* maybe */
```

This routine is often best called as a subroutine. The residual line count is then available in the variable RESULT.

Examples:

```
Call LINEOUT 'Output file','Hello'
Call LINEOUT 'A:rexx.bat','Shell',12
Call LINEOUT ,'Hello'
```

Note: If the lines are to be written to the default output stream and no error is possible, then the SAY instruction would usually be used instead.

LINES([name])

returns the number of complete lines remaining in the character input stream *name*. If the stream has already been read with the CHARIN function, this may include an initial partial line. In the case of persistent streams the count starts at the current read position. (See page 139 for a discussion of the REXX input/output model.)

The form of the *name* is implementation-dependent. If *name* is omitted, then the number of complete lines available in the default input stream is returned.

If an implementation cannot determine the count accurately or efficiently, then it may return 1 for any non-zero count or when the count is unknown. An actual line count may therefore be used only in programs specific to a particular environment in which LINES is fully supported for the specified stream.

Examples:

```
LINES(myfile)   == 7  /* perhaps */
LINES(nonfile)  == 0  /* perhaps */
LINES()         == 2  /* perhaps */
```

Note: The CHARS function may be used to return the number of characters (rather than lines) remaining in the stream.

MAX(number[,number]...)

returns the largest number from the given list of numbers – that is, the first number in the list which is equal to the result of adding a positive number or zero to any of the other numbers in the list. The result is formatted according to the current NUMERIC settings.

Examples:

```
MAX(12,6,7,9)       == 12
MAX(17.3,19,17.03)  == 19
MAX(-7,-3,-4.3)     == -3
```

MIN(number[,number]...)

returns the smallest number from the given list of numbers – that is, the first number in the list which is equal to the result of subtracting a positive number or zero from any of the other numbers in the list. The result is formatted according to the current NUMERIC settings.

Examples:

```
MIN(12,6,7,9)       == 6
MIN(17.3,19,17.03)  == 17.03
MIN(-7,-3,-4.3)     == -7
```

OVERLAY(new,target[,[n][,[length][,pad]]])

overlays the string *new*, padded or truncated to length *length*, onto the string *target* starting at the nth character. If *length* is specified it must be positive or zero. If n is greater than the length of the target string, padding is added before the *new* string also. The default *pad* character is a blank, and the default value for n is 1. n must be greater than 0. The default value for *length* is the length of *new*.

Examples:

```
OVERLAY(' ','abcdef',3)       == 'ab def'
OVERLAY('.','abcdef',3,2)     == 'ab. ef'
OVERLAY('qq','abcd')          == 'qqcd'
OVERLAY('qq','abcd',4)        == 'abcqq'
OVERLAY('123','abc',5,6,'+')  == 'abc+123+++'
```

POS(needle,haystack[,start])

returns the position of one string, *needle*, in another, *haystack*. (See also the LASTPOS function.) If the string *needle* is not found, or is the null string, 0 is returned. By default the search starts at the first character of *haystack* (that is, *start* has the value 1). This may be overridden by specifying *start* (which must be positive), the point at which to start the search.

Examples:

```
POS('day','Saturday')     == 6
POS('x','abc def ghi')    == 0
POS(' ','abc def ghi')    == 4
POS(' ','abc def ghi',5)  == 8
```

QUEUED()

returns the number of lines remaining in the external data queue when the function is invoked. (See page 139 for a discussion of the REXX input/output model.)

Example:

```
QUEUED() == 5    /* perhaps */
```

RANDOM([min][,[max][,seed]])

or

RANDOM(max)

returns a quasi-random non-negative whole number in the range *min* to *max* inclusive. If only the first argument is specified it is taken as a maximum, and the range will be from 0 through that number. If no arguments or more than one argument are specified, the default values for *min* and *max* are 0 and 999 respectively. A specific *seed* (which must be a whole number) for the random number may be given as the third argument to start a repeatable sequence of results.

The magnitude of the range (that is, *max* minus *min*) may not exceed 100000.

Examples:

```
/* Possible results might be: */
RANDOM()        == 305
RANDOM(5,8)     == 7
RANDOM(,,1989)  == 420  /* reproducible */
RANDOM(2)       == 0
```

Notes:

1. To obtain a predictable sequence of quasi-random numbers, call RANDOM a number of times, but only specify a *seed* on the first call. For example, to simulate ten throws of a six-sided dice:

```
/* Start by invoking with any number for seed */
say random(1,6,12345)
do 9
  say random(1,6)
  end
```

The numbers are generated mathematically, using the initial *seed*, so that as far as possible they appear to be random. Running the program again will produce the same sequence; using a different initial *seed* will almost always produce a different sequence. If you do not supply a *seed*, then the first time RANDOM is called an arbitrary (and probably time-varying) seed will be used. Typically it will be derived from the time-of-day clock, and hence your program will almost always give different results each time it is run.

2.   The random number generator is global for an entire program – the current seed is not saved across internal routine calls.

3.   The actual random number generator used may differ from implementation to implementation.

REVERSE(string)

returns *string*, swapped end for end.

Examples:

```
REVERSE('ABc.')         ==  '.cBA'
REVERSE('XYZ ')         ==  ' ZYX'
REVERSE('Tranquility')  ==  'ytiliuqnarT'
```

RIGHT(string,length[,pad])

returns a string of length *length* containing the right-most *length* characters of *string* – that is, padded with *pad* characters (or truncated) on the left as needed. The default *pad* character is a blank. *length* must be non-negative.

Examples:

```
RIGHT('abc  d',8)  ==  '   abc  d'
RIGHT('abc def',5)  ==  'c def'
RIGHT('12',5,'0')   ==  '00012'
```

SIGN(number)

returns a number that indicates the sign of *number*. If the number is less than 0 then '-1' is returned; if it is 0 then '0' is returned; and if it is greater than 0 then '1' is returned.

Examples:

```
SIGN('12.3')    ==  1
SIGN(0.0)       ==  0
SIGN(' -0.307') ==  -1
```

SOURCELINE([n])

If *n* is omitted, returns the line number of the final line in the program, or 0 if no source lines are available.

If *n* is given, the *n*th line in the program is returned, if available at the time of execution (otherwise the null string is returned).

n must be a positive whole number, and must not exceed the number returned by a call to SOURCELINE with no arguments.

Examples:

```
SOURCELINE()  == 10
SOURCELINE(1) == '/* A 10-line program */'
```

SPACE(string[,[n][,pad]])

formats the blank-delimited words in *string* with *n* (and only *n*) *pad* characters between each word. *n* must be non-negative. If it is 0, all blanks are removed. Leading and trailing blanks are always removed. The default for *n* is 1, and the default *pad* character is a blank.

Examples:

```
SPACE('abc   def  ')       == 'abc def'
SPACE('  abc def',3)       == 'abc   def'
SPACE('abc   def  ',1)     == 'abc def'
SPACE('abc   def  ',0)     == 'abcdef'
SPACE('abc   def  ',2,'+') == 'abc++def'
```

STREAM(name[,operation[,streamcommand]])

returns a string describing the state of, or the result of an operation upon, the character stream *name*. (See page 139 for a discussion of the REXX input/output model.)

This function is used to request information on the state of an input or output stream, or to carry out some particular implementation-dependent operation on the stream. The first argument, *name*, specifies the stream to which the function refers – the form of this name is implementation-dependent. The second argument may be one of the following *operation* strings (of which only the first letter is needed) which describes the action to be carried out:

C   (Command); an operation, specified by the *streamcommand* given as the third argument, is applied to the selected input or output stream. The stream command string describes an implementation-dependent command that may be necessary or useful for certain operating environments but which may not be applicable for all REXX implementations (for example, the operation of opening, closing, or committing a change to a stream). The returned string will depend on the operation performed, and may be the null string.

D   (Description); returns any implementation-dependent descriptive string associated with the current state of the stream. If none is available the null string is returned. *streamcommand* must not be supplied.

S   (State); returns an indication of the current state of the specified stream. This is the default operation; *streamcommand* must not be supplied. One of the following is returned:

ERROR
> The stream has been subject to an erroneous operation (possibly during input, output, or via the STREAM function – see page 142). Additional information about the error may be available by invoking the STREAM function with a request for the implementation-dependent description.

NOTREADY
> The stream is known to be in a state such that normal input or output operations attempted upon it would raise the NOTREADY condition (see page 142). For example, a simple input stream may have a defined length; an attempt to read that stream (with the CHARIN or LINEIN built-in functions, perhaps) beyond that limit may make the stream unavailable until some operation resets the state of the stream.

READY
> The stream is known to be in a state such that normal input ot output operations may be attempted (this is the usual state for a stream, though it does not guarantee that any particular operation will succeed).

UNKNOWN
> The state of the stream is unknown. This response is used when the state of the stream cannot be determined. For example, in some operating environments, the state of the stream can only be determined by carrying out some operation on the stream – this operation might have a side-effect that alters the state of the stream, and so the state will only be known after that operation has been carried out.

Examples:

```
/* Possible results might be: */
STREAM(myfile)              == 'READY'
STREAM(readitall)           == 'ERROR'
STREAM(readitall,'D')       == 'END INPUT'
STREAM(myfile,'C','SHARE')  == 'SHARED BY 5'
```

Note: The state (and operation) of an input or output stream is external to a REXX program, in that it is not saved and restored across internal function and subroutine calls (including those caused by a CALL ON condition trap).

STRIP(string[,[option][,char]])

removes Leading, Trailing, or Both leading and trailing characters from *string* when the first character of *option* is L, T, or B respectively (these may be given in either upper case or lower case). The default is B. The third argument, *char*, specifies the character to be removed, with the default being a blank. If given, *char* must be exactly one character long.

Examples:

```
STRIP('  ab c  ')       == 'ab c'
STRIP('  ab c  ','L') == 'ab c  '
STRIP('  ab c  ','t') == '  ab c'
STRIP('12.7000',,0)   == '12.7'
STRIP('0012.700',,0)  == '12.7'
```

SUBSTR(string,n[,[length][,pad]])

returns the sub-string of *string* that begins at the nth character, and is of length *length*, padded with *pad* characters if necessary. *n* must be positive. If *n* is greater than LENGTH(*string*), then only pad characters can be returned.

If *length* is omitted it defaults to be the rest of the string. The default *pad* character is a blank.

Examples:

```
SUBSTR('abc',2)       == 'bc'
SUBSTR('abc',2,4)     == 'bc  '
SUBSTR('abc',2,6,'.') == 'bc....'
```

Note: In some situations the positional (numeric) patterns of parsing templates are more convenient for selecting sub-strings, especially if more than one sub-string is to be extracted from a string. See also the LEFT and RIGHT functions.

SUBWORD(string,n[,length])

returns the sub-string of *string* that starts at the nth word, and is up to *length* blank-delimited words long. *n* must be positive. If *length* is omitted it defaults to be the remaining words in the string. The returned string will never have leading or trailing blanks, but will include all blanks between the selected words.

Examples:

```
SUBWORD('Now is the  time',2,2) == 'is the'
SUBWORD('Now is the  time',3)   == 'the  time'
SUBWORD('Now is the  time',5)   == ''
```

SYMBOL(name)

returns the state of the symbol named by *name*. If *name* is not a valid REXX symbol, `'BAD'` is returned. If it is the name of a variable (that is, a symbol that has been assigned a value), `'VAR'` is returned. Otherwise `'LIT'` is returned, which indicates that it is either a constant symbol or a symbol that has not yet been assigned a value (that is, a Literal).

Like symbols appearing normally in REXX expressions, lower case characters in the name will be translated to upper case and substitution in a compound name will occur if possible.

Note: Normally *name* should be specified as a literal string (or derived from an expression), to prevent substitution by its value before it is passed to the function.

Examples:

```
/* Following: Drop A.3; J=3   */
SYMBOL('J')   == 'VAR'
SYMBOL(J)     == 'LIT'   /* has tested "3"       */
SYMBOL('a.j') == 'LIT'   /* has tested "A.3"     */
SYMBOL(2)     == 'LIT'   /* a constant symbol */
SYMBOL('*')   == 'BAD'   /* an invalid symbol */
```

TIME([option])

by default returns the local time in the 24-hour clock format `'hh:mm:ss'` (hours, minutes, and seconds); for example, `'04:41:37'`.

The following *option* strings (of which only the first letter is significant) may be supplied to obtain alternative formats, or to gain access to the elapsed time clock.

C   (Civil); returns `'hh:mmxx'`, the time in Civil format, in which the hours may take the values 1 through 12, and the minutes the values 00 through 59. The minutes are followed immediately by the letters "am" or "pm" to distinguish times in the morning (midnight 12:00am through 11:59am) from noon and afternoon (noon 12:00pm through 11:59pm). The hour will not have a leading zero. The minute field shows the current minute (rather than the nearest minute) for consistency with other TIME results.

E   (Elapsed); returns `'sssssssss.uuuuuu'`, the number of seconds (and microseconds) since the elapsed time clock was started or reset (see below). The number will have no leading zeros or blanks, and is not affected by the setting of NUMERIC DIGITS. The fractional part will always have six digits.

H   (Hours); returns the number of completed hours since midnight in the format `'hh'` (no leading zeros or blanks, except for a result of `'0'`).

L   (Long); returns the time in the format   'hh:mm:ss.uuuuuu' (uuuuuu is the fraction of seconds, in microseconds). The first eight characters of the result follow the same rules as for the Normal form, and the fractional part will always be six characters.

M   (Minutes); returns the number of completed minutes since midnight in the format 'mmmm' (no leading zeros or blanks, except for a result of '0').

N   (Normal); explicitly returns the time in the default format 'hh:mm:ss', as described above. The hours may take the values 00 through 23, and minutes and seconds may take 00 through 59; these are all always two digits. Any fractions of seconds are ignored (times are never rounded up).

R   (Reset); returns 'sssssssss.uuuuuu', the number of sec-onds.microseconds since the elapsed time clock was started or reset (see below), and also simultaneously resets the elapsed time clock to zero. The number will have no leading zeros or blanks, and is not affected by the setting of NUMERIC DIGITS. The fractional part will always have six digits.

S   (Seconds); returns number of completed seconds since midnight in the format 'sssss' (no leading zeros or blanks, except for a result of '0').

Examples:

```
TIME()      == '16:54:22'              /* perhaps */
TIME('C')   == '4:54pm'
TIME('H')   == 16
TIME('L')   == '16:54:22.123456'
TIME('M')   == 1014                    /* 54 + 60*16 */
TIME('n')   == '16:54:22'
TIME('s')   == 60862              /* 22+60*(54+60*16) */
```

The elapsed time clock

The TIME function may be used for measuring real (elapsed) time intervals. On the first call in a program to TIME('E') or TIME('R'), the elapsed time clock is started and either call would return 0. From then on, calls to TIME('E') and to TIME('R') will return the elapsed time since that first call or since the last call to TIME('R').

An example of the elapsed time calculator:

```
TIME('E')  == 0          /* The first call */
/* pause of one second here */
TIME('E')  == 1.002345   /* or thereabouts */
/* pause of one second here */
TIME('R')  == 2.004690   /* or thereabouts */
/* pause of one second here */
TIME('R')  == 1.002345   /* or thereabouts */
```

The clock is saved across internal routine calls, which is to say that an internal routine will inherit the time clock started by its caller, but if it should reset the clock then any timing being done by the caller will not be affected.

Note: See the note under DATE about the consistency of times within a single clause. The elapsed time clock is synchronized to the other calls to TIME and DATE, so multiple calls to the elapsed time clock in a single clause will always return the same result. Since the clock is synchronized, the interval between two normal TIME/DATE results may be calculated exactly using the elapsed time clock.

Implementation minimum: An elapsed time counter of at least 9 digits in seconds (equivalent to over 31.6 years) should be supported. The fractional part of the seconds should, if possible, provide at least millisecond precision, with any remaining digits being set to 0.

TRACE([setting])

returns the trace setting currently in effect, and optionally alters the setting.

If *setting* is supplied, it is used to select the trace setting. The *setting* must be a valid prefix ("?") and/or one of the alphabetic character settings (*i.e.*, starting with A, C, E, F, I, L, N, O, or R) associated with the TRACE instruction. See the TRACE instruction, on page 73, for details.

Unlike the TRACE instruction, the TRACE function alters the trace action even if interactive tracing is active. Also unlike the TRACE instruction, *setting* may not be a number.

Examples:

```
TRACE()     == '?R' /* maybe */
TRACE('O')  == '?R' /* also sets tracing off */
TRACE('?A') == 'O'  /* now interactive */
```

TRANSLATE(string[,[tableo][,[tablei][,pad]]])

returns the characters in *string* with each character either unchanged or translated to another character.

The TRANSLATE function acts by searching the input translate table, *tablei*, for each character in *string*. If the character is found (the first (leftmost) occurrence being used if there are duplicates) then the corresponding character in the output translate table, *tableo*, is used in the result string; otherwise the original character found in *string* is used. The result string is always the same length as *string*.

If neither translate table is given, *string* is simply translated to upper case. Otherwise, the translate tables may be of any length. The input translate table defaults to XRANGE('00'x, 'FF'x). The output table defaults to the null string, and is padded with *pad* or truncated as necessary to be the same length as *tablei*. The default *pad* is a blank.

Examples:

```
TRANSLATE('abcdef')                 ==  'ABCDEF'
TRANSLATE('abbc','&','b')           ==  'a&&c'
TRANSLATE('abcdef','12','ec')       ==  'ab2d1f'
TRANSLATE('abcdef','12','abcd','.') ==  '12..ef'
TRANSLATE('4123','abcd','1234')     ==  'dabc'
```

Note: The last example shows how the TRANSLATE function may be used to reorder the characters in a string. In the example any 4-character string could be specified as the second argument and its last character would be moved to the beginning of the string.

TRUNC(number[,n])

returns the integer part of the number, and *n* decimal places (digits after the decimal point). *n* must be non-negative, and defaults to zero. The *number* is first rounded according to standard REXX rules, just as though the operation "number+0" had been carried out. The number is then truncated to *n* decimal places (or trailing zeros are added if needed to make up the specified length). If *n* is 0 (the default) then an integer with no decimal point is returned. The result will never be in exponential form.

Examples:

```
TRUNC(12.3)         == 12
TRUNC(127.09782,3)  == 127.097
TRUNC(127.1,3)      == 127.100
TRUNC(127,2)        == 127.00
```

VALUE(name[,[newvalue]][,selector])

returns the value of the symbol named by *name* (which often will be constructed dynamically), and optionally assigns it a new value. By default, the function refers to the current REXX variables environment, but other, external, collections of variables may be selected. If the function is used to refer to REXX variables, then *name* must be a valid REXX symbol,[38] and (as with symbols used in REXX expressions) lower case characters in the name will be translated to upper case and substitution in a compound name will occur if possible.

If *newvalue* is supplied, then the named variable is assigned this new value. This does not change the the result returned by the function, which will be the value as it was before the assignment.

Examples:

```
/* After:                                        */
/* Drop A3; A33=7; K=3; fred='K'; list.5='?' */
VALUE('a'k)        == 'A3'
VALUE('a'k||k)     == '7'
VALUE('fred')      == 'K'   /* looks up FRED       */
VALUE(fred)        == '3'   /* looks up K          */
VALUE(fred,5)      == '3'   /* and sets K=5        */
VALUE(fred)        == '5'
VALUE('LIST.'k)    == '?'   /* looks up LIST.5     */
```

The VALUE function may be used to access external collections of variables (sometimes called *pools*); *selector*, if specified, names an implementation-defined external collection of variables (if the specified external collection does not exist, an error results). In this case, *name* does not have to be a valid REXX symbol; if the name is invalid for the specified collection of variables, then the action taken is implementation-defined (as appropriate for the particular collection of variables). As before, if *newvalue* is specified then the named variable is assigned this new value, without affecting the result of the function.

Examples:

```
/* Possible results might be: */
/* Look up and set "toy" in SHARED pool */
VALUE('toy','Buxton','SHARED')   == 'Calistoga'
/* Look up "toy" in SHARED pool */
VALUE('toy',,'SHARED')           == 'Buxton'
/* Look up "toy" in SYSTEM pool */
VALUE('toy',,'SYSTEM')           == 'Bath Spa'
```

---

[38] The SYMBOL function may be used to test for the validity of a symbol, and takes the same form of *name*.

Notes:

1. If the VALUE function refers to an uninitialized REXX variable then the default value of the variable is always returned; the NOVALUE condition is not raised. NOVALUE is never raised by a reference to an external collection of variables.

2. If the *name* is specified as a single literal string and neither of the other arguments is given, the symbol is a constant and so the whole function call could usually be replaced directly by the string between the quotes. (For example, "fred=VALUE('k');" is identical to the assignment "fred=k;", unless the NOVALUE condition is being trapped – see page 145.)

VERIFY(string,reference[,[option][,start]])

verifies that the *string* is composed only of characters from *reference*, by returning the position of the first character in *string* that is not also in *reference*. If all the characters were found in *reference*, 0 is returned.

The *option* may be either 'Nomatch' (the default) or 'Match'. Only the first character of *option* is significant and it may be in upper case or in lower case, as usual. If 'Match' is specified, the position of the first character in *string* that **is** in *reference* is returned, or 0 if none of the characters were found.

The default for *start* is 1, *i.e.*, the search starts at the first character of *string*. This can be overridden by giving a different *start* point, which must be positive.

If *string* is null, the function returns 0, regardless of the value of the third argument. Similarly if *start* is greater than LENGTH(*string*), 0 is returned.

If *reference* is null, then the returned value is the value used for *start*, unless 'Match' is specified (in which case 0 is returned).

Examples:

```
VERIFY('123','1234567890')          == 0
VERIFY('1Z3','1234567890')          == 2
VERIFY('AB4T','1234567890','M')     == 3
VERIFY('1P3Q4','1234567890',,3)     == 4
VERIFY('ABCDE','',,3)               == 3
VERIFY('AB3CD5','1234567890','M',4) == 6
```

WORD(string,n)

> returns the nth blank-delimited word in *string*. *n* must be positive. If there are fewer than *n* words in *string*, the null string is returned. This function is exactly equivalent to SUBWORD (*string,n,*1).

> **Examples:**

```
WORD('Now is the time',3) == 'the'
WORD('Now is the time',5) == ''
```

WORDINDEX(string,n)

> returns the character position of the nth blank-delimited word in *string*. *n* must be positive. If there are fewer than *n* words in the string, 0 is returned.

> **Examples:**

```
WORDINDEX('Now is the time',3) == 8
WORDINDEX('Now is the time',6) == 0
```

WORDLENGTH(string,n)

> returns the length of the nth blank-delimited word in *string*. *n* must be positive. If there are fewer than *n* words in the string, 0 is returned.

> **Examples:**

```
WORDLENGTH('Now is the time',2)    == 2
WORDLENGTH('Now comes the time',2) == 5
WORDLENGTH('Now is the time',6)    == 0
```

WORDPOS(phrase,string[,start])

> searches *string* for the first occurrence of the sequence of blank-delimited words *phrase*, and returns the word number of the first word of *phrase* in *string*. Multiple blanks between words in either *phrase* or *string* are treated as a single blank for the comparison, but otherwise the words must match exactly. If *phrase* is not found, or contains no words, 0 is returned.

> By default the search starts at the first word in *string*. This may be overridden by specifying *start* (which must be. positive), the word at which to start the search.

Examples:

```
WORDPOS('the','now is the time')          == 3
WORDPOS('The','now is the time')          == 0
WORDPOS('is the','now is the time')       == 2
WORDPOS('is   the','now is the time')     == 2
WORDPOS('is  time ','now is  the time')   == 0
WORDPOS('be','To be or not to be')        == 2
WORDPOS('be','To be or not to be',3)      == 6
```

WORDS(string)

returns the number of blank-delimited words in *string*.

Examples:

```
WORDS('Now is the time') == 4
WORDS(' ')               == 0
```

XRANGE([start][,end])

returns a string of all valid character encodings, in ascending order, between and including the characters *start* and *end*. *start* defaults to '00'x, and *end* defaults to 'FF'x. If *start* is greater than *end*, the values will wrap from 'FF'x to '00'x. *start* and *end* must be single characters.

Examples:

```
XRANGE('a','f')     == 'abcdef'
XRANGE('03'x,'07'x) == '0304050607'x
XRANGE(,'04'x)      == '0001020304'x
XRANGE('FE'x,'02'x) == 'FEFF000102'x
```

X2B(hex-string)

Hexadecimal to Binary. Converts *hex-string* (a string of hexadecimal characters) to an equivalent string of binary digits. *hex-string* may be of any length; each hexadecimal character with be converted to a string of four binary digits. The returned string will have a length that is a multiple of four, and will not include any blanks.

hex-string may be the null string, in which case a null string is returned.

Blanks may optionally be included in *hex-string* (at byte boundaries only, not leading or trailing) to aid readability; they are ignored.

Examples:

```
X2B('C3')    == '11000011'
X2B('7')     == '0111'
X2B('1 C1')  == '000111000001'
```

X2B may be combined with the D2X or C2X functions to convert numbers or character strings to binary form.

Examples:

```
X2B(C2X('C3'x))   == '11000011'
X2B(D2X('129'))   == '10000001'
X2B(D2X('12'))    == '1100'
```

X2C(hex-string)

Hexadecimal to Character. Converts *hex-string* (a string of hexadecimal characters) to character (packs). *hex-string* may be of any length and will be padded with a leading 0 if necessary to make an even number of hexadecimal digits.

hex-string may be the null string, in which case a null string is returned.

Blanks may optionally be included in *hex-string* (at byte boundaries only, not leading or trailing) to aid readability; they are ignored.

Examples:

```
X2C('F7F2 A2') == '72s'
X2C('F7f2a2')  == '72s'
X2C('F')       == '0F'x
```

X2D(hex-string[,n])

Hexadecimal to Decimal. Converts *hex-string* (a string of hexadecimal characters) to decimal. If the result cannot be expressed as a whole number, an error results – that is, the result must have no more digits than the setting of NUMERIC DIGITS. *hex-string* may be the null string, in which case '0' is returned.

Blanks may optionally be included in *hex-string* (at byte boundaries only, not leading or trailing) to aid readability; they are ignored.

If *n* is not specified, *hex-string* is taken to be an unsigned number.

Examples:

```
X2D('0E')     == 14
X2D('81')     == 129
X2D('F81')    == 3969
X2D('FF81')   == 65409
X2D('c6 f0'X) == 240
```

If *n* is specified, the string is taken as a signed number expressed in *n* hexadecimal characters. If the most significant (left-most) bit is zero then the number is positive; otherwise it is a negative number in two's complement form. In both cases it is converted to a REXX whole number which may, therefore, be negative. If *n* is 0, 0 is always returned.

If necessary, *hex-string* is padded on the left with 0 characters (note, not "sign-extended"), or truncated on the left, to length *n* characters; (that is, as though RIGHT(*string,n,*'0') had been executed.)

Examples:

```
X2D('81',2)   == -127
X2D('81',4)   == 129
X2D('F081',4) == -3967
X2D('F081',3) == 129
X2D('F081',2) == -127
X2D('F081',1) == 1
X2D('0031',0) == 0
```

See also the C2D function.

SECTION 10:   PARSING FOR ARG, PARSE, AND PULL

Three instructions (ARG, PARSE, and PULL) allow a selected string to be parsed (split up) and assigned to variables, under the control of a *template*. The various mechanisms in the template allow a string to be split up by words (delimited by blanks), or by explicit matching of strings (called *patterns*), or by specifying numeric positions (*positional patterns*) – for example, to extract data from particular columns of a line read from a character stream.

This section first gives some informal examples of how the parsing template can be used, then describes in more detail the mechanisms used.

Introduction to parsing

The simplest form of parsing template consists of a list of variable names. The string being parsed is split up into words (characters delimited by blanks), and each word from the string is assigned to a variable in sequence from left to right. The final variable is treated specially in that it will be assigned whatever is left of the original string and may therefore contain several words. For example, in the PARSE instruction

```
parse value 'This is a sentence.' with  v1 v2 v3
```

V1 would be assigned the value "This", V2 would be assigned the value "is", and V3 would be assigned the value "a sentence.".

Leading blanks are removed from each word in the string before it is assigned to a variable, as is the blank that delimits the end of the word. Thus variables set in this manner (V1 and V2 in the example) will never have leading or trailing blanks, though V3 could have both leading and trailing blanks. In addition, if PARSE UPPER (or the ARG or PULL instruction) is used, the whole string is translated into upper case before parsing begins.

Note that the variables mentioned in a template are always given a new value and so if there are fewer words in the string than variables in the template then the unused variables will be set to null.

A literal string may be used in a template as a pattern to split up the string. For example

```
parse value 'To be, or not to be?' with  w1 ',' w2
```

would cause the string to be scanned for the comma, and then split at that point: thus W1 would be set to "To be", and W2 is set to " or not to be?". Note that the pattern itself (and **only** the pattern) is removed from the string. In fact each section is treated in just the same way as the whole string was in the previous example, and so either section may be split up into words.

Thus, in:

```
parse value 'To be, or not to be?' with  w1 ',' w2 w3 w4
```

W2 and W3 would be assigned the values "or" and "not", and W4 would be assigned the remainder: "to be?". If UPPER was specified on the instruction, then all the results would be in upper case.

If the string in the previous example did not contain a comma, then the pattern would effectively "match" the end of the string, so the variable to the left of the pattern would get the entire input string, and the variables to the right would be set to null.

The pattern may be specified as a variable, by putting the variable name in parentheses. The following instructions therefore have the same effect as the last example:

```
c=','
parse value 'To be, or not to be?' with  w1 (c) w2 w3 w4
```

The third kind of parsing mechanism is the numeric positional pattern. This works in the same way as the string pattern except that it specifies a column number. So:

```
parse value 'Flying pigs have wings' with  x1 5 x2
```

would split the string at column 5, so X1 would be "Flyi" and X2 would start at column 5 and so be "ng pigs have wings".

More than one pattern is allowed, so for example:

```
parse value 'Flying pigs have wings' with  x1 5 x2 10 x3
```

would split the string at columns 5 and 10, so X2 would be "ng pi" and X3 would be "gs have wings".

The numbers can be relative to the last number used, so

```
parse value 'Flying pigs have wings' with  x1 5 x2 +5 x3
```

would have exactly the same effect as the last example: here the "+5" may be thought of as specifying the length of the string to be assigned to X2.

As with literal string patterns, the positional patterns can be specified as a variable by putting the name of a variable, in parentheses, in place of the number. An absolute column number can be indicated by using an equals sign ("=") instead of a plus or minus sign. The last example could therefore be written

```
start=5
length=5
data='Flying pigs have wings'
parse var data  x1 =(start) x2 +(length) x3
```

String patterns and positional patterns can be mixed (in effect the beginning of a string pattern just specifies a variable column number) and some very powerful things can be done with templates. The next section describes in more detail how the various mechanisms interact.

Finally, it is possible to parse more than one string. An internal function or subroutine may have more than one argument string, for example. To get at each string in turn, you just put a comma in the parsing template, so if the invocation of the function FRED was:

```
fred('This is the first string',2)
```

then the instruction

```
parse arg first, second
```

would put the string 'This is the first string' into the variable FIRST, and the string '2' into the variable SECOND. Between the commas you can put any normal template with patterns (and so on) to do more complex parsing on each of the argument strings.

Parsing definition

This section describes the rules that govern parsing.

In its most general form, a template consists of alternating pattern specifications and variable names. Blanks may be added between patterns and variable names to separate the tokens and to improve readability. The patterns and variable names are used strictly in sequence from left to right, and are used once only. In practice, various simpler forms are used in which either variable names or patterns may be omitted: we can therefore have variable names without patterns in between, and patterns without intervening variable names.

In general, the value assigned to a variable is that sequence of characters in the input string between the point that is matched by the pattern on its left and the point that is matched by the pattern on its right.

If the first item in a template is a variable, then there is an implicit pattern on the left that matches the start of the string, and similarly if the last item in a template is a variable then there is an implicit pattern on the right that matches the end of the string. Hence the simplest template consists of a single variable name which in this case is assigned the entire input string.

Setting a variable during parsing is identical to setting a variable in an assignment. It is therefore possible to set an entire collection of compound variables during parsing. (See pages 32 and 35.)

The constructs that may appear as patterns fall into two categories; patterns that act by searching for a matching string (literal patterns), and numeric patterns that specify an absolute or relative position in the string (positional patterns). Either of these can be specified explicitly in the template, or alternatively by a reference to a variable whose value is to be used as the pattern.

For the following examples, assume that the following sample string is being parsed; note that all blanks are significant – there are two blanks after the first word "is" and also after the second comma:

```
'This is  the text which, I think,  is scanned.'
```

Parsing with literal patterns

Literal patterns cause scanning of the data string to find a sequence that matches the value of the literal. Literals are expressed as a quoted string. The null string matches the end of the data.

The template:

```
w1 ',' w2 ',' rest
```

when parsing the sample string, results in:

```
W1   has the value "This is  the text which"
W2   has the value " I think"
REST has the value "  is scanned."
```

Here the string is parsed using a template that asks that each of the variables receive a value corresponding to a portion of the original string between commas; the commas are given as quoted strings. Note that the patterns themselves are removed from the data being parsed.

A different parse would result with the template:

```
w1 ',' w2 ',' w3 ',' rest
```

which would result in:

```
W1   has the value "This is  the text which"
W2   has the value " I think"
W3   has the value "  is scanned."
REST has the value ""  (null)
```

This illustrates an important rule. When a match for a pattern cannot be found in the input string, it instead "matches" the end of the string. Thus, no match was found for the third ',' in the template, and so W3 was assigned the rest of the string. REST was assigned a null value because the pattern on its left had already reached the end of the string.

Note that **all** variables that appear in a template in this way are assigned a new value.

Parsing strings into words

If a variable is directly followed by one or more other variables, then the string selected by the patterns is assigned to the variables in the following manner. Each blank-delimited word in the string is assigned to each variable in turn, except for the last variable in the group (which is assigned the remainder of the string). The values of the variables which are assigned words will have neither leading nor trailing blanks.

Thus the template:

```
w1 w2 w3 rest ','
```

would result in:

```
W1    has the value "This'
W2    has the value "is"
W3    has the value "the"
REST has the value "text which"
```

Note that the final variable (REST in this example) could have had both leading blanks and trailing blanks, since only the blank that delimits the previous word is removed from the data.

Also observe that this example is not the same as specifying explicit blanks as patterns, as the template:

```
w1 ' ' w2 ' ' w3 ' ' rest ','
```

would in fact result in:

```
W1    has the value "This'
W2    has the value "is"
W3    has the value ""   (null)
REST has the value "the text which"
```

since the third pattern would match the third blank in the data.

In general, when a variable is followed by another variable then parsing of the input into individual words is implied. The parsing process may be thought of as first splitting the original string up into other strings using the various kinds of patterns, and then assigning each of these new strings to (zero or more) variables.

Use of the period as a placeholder

The symbol consisting of a single period acts as a placeholder in a template. It has exactly the same effect as a variable name, except that no variable is set. It is especially useful as a "dummy variable" in a list of variables, or to collect (ignore) unwanted information at the end of a string. Thus the template:

```
. . . word4 .
```

would extract the fourth word (`'text'`) from the sample string and place it in the variable WORD4.

Parsing with positional patterns

Positional patterns may be used to cause the parsing to occur on the basis of position within the string, rather than on its contents. They take the form of whole numbers, optionally preceded by a plus, minus, or equals sign which indicate relative or absolute positioning. These may cause the matching operation to "back up" to an earlier position in the data string, which can only occur when positional patterns are used.

Absolute positional patterns: A number in a template that is **not** preceded by a sign refers to a particular (absolute) character column in the input, with 1 referring to the first column. For example, the template

```
s1 10 s2 20 s3
```

results in

```
S1 has the value "This is  "
S2 has the value "the text w"
S3 has the value "hich, I think,  is scanned."
```

Here S1 is assigned characters from the first through the ninth character, and S2 receives input characters 10 through 19. As usual the final variable, S3, is assigned the remainder of the input. An equals sign ("=") may be placed before the number to indicate explicitly that it is to be used as an absolute column position; the last template could have been written

```
s1 =10 s2 =20 s3
```

A positional pattern that has no sign or is preceded by the equals sign is known as an *absolute positional pattern*.

Relative positional patterns: A number in a template that is preceded by a plus or minus sign indicates movement relative to the character position at which the previous pattern match occurred. This is a *relative positional pattern*.

If a plus or minus is specified, then the position used for the next match is calculated by adding (or subtracting) the number given to the last matched position. The last matched position is the position of the first character of the last match, whether specified numerically or by a string. For example, the instructions:

```
a = '123456789'
parse var a  3 w1 +3 w2 3 w3
```

result in

```
W1 has the value "345"
W2 has the value "6789"
W3 has the value "3456789"
```

The +3 in this case is equivalent to the absolute number 6 in the same position, and may also be considered to be specifying the length of the data string to be assigned to the variable W1.

This example also illustrates the effects of a positional pattern that implies movement to a character position to the left of (or to) the point at which the last match occurred. The variable on the left is assigned characters through the end of the input, and the variable on the right is, as usual, assigned characters starting at the position dictated by the pattern.

A useful effect of this is that multiple assignments can be made:

```
parse var x 1 w1 1 w2 1 w3
```

results in assigning the (entire) value of X to W1, W2, and W3. (The first "1" here could be omitted as it is effectively the same as the implicit starting pattern described at the beginning of this section.)

If a positional pattern specifies a column that is greater than the length of the data, it is equivalent to specifying the end of the data (*i.e.*, no padding takes place). Similarly, if a pattern specifies a column to the left of the first column of the data, this is not an error but instead is taken to specify the first column of the data.

Any pattern match sets the "last position" in a string to which a relative positional pattern can refer. The "last position" set by a literal pattern is the position at which the match occurred, that is, the position in the data of the *first* character in the pattern. The literal pattern in this case is **not** removed from the parsed data. Thus the template:

```
',' -1 x +1
```

will:

1. Find the first comma in the input (or the end of the string if there is no comma).

2. Back up one position.

3. Assign one character (the character immediately preceding the comma or end of string) to the variable X.

One possible application of this is looking for abbreviations in a string. Thus the instruction:

```
/* Ensure options have leading blank & are upper case */
parse upper value ' 'opts with ' PR' +1 prword ' '
```

will set the variable PRWORD to the first word in OPTS that starts with "PR" or will set it to null if no such word exists.

Notes:

1. The positional pattern +0 is valid, and may be used to include the whole of a previous literal (or variable) pattern within the data string to be parsed into any following variables.

2. As illustrated in the last example, patterns may follow each other in the template without intervening variable names. In this case each pattern is obeyed in turn from left to right, as usual.

3. There may be blanks between the sign in a positional pattern and the number, because REXX defines that blanks adjacent to special characters are removed.

Parsing with variable patterns

It is sometimes desirable to be able to specify a pattern by using the value of a variable instead of a fixed string or number. This may be achieved by placing the name of the variable to be used as the pattern in parentheses (blanks are not necessary either inside or outside the parentheses, but may be added if desired). This is called a *variable reference*.

If the parenthesis to the left of the variable name is not preceded by an equals, plus, or minus sign ("=", "+", or "-") the value of the variable is then used as though it were a literal (string) pattern. The variable may be one that has been set earlier in the parsing process, so for example:

```
input="L/look for/1 10"
parse var input  verb 2 delim +1 string (delim) rest
```

will set:

```
VERB   = 'L'
DELIM  = '/'
STRING = 'look for'
REST   = '1 10'
```

If the left parenthesis **is** preceded by an equals, plus, or minus sign then the value of the variable is used as an absolute or relative positional pattern (instead of as a literal string pattern). In this case the value of the variable must be a non-negative whole number, and (as before) it may have been set earlier in the parsing process.

Parsing multiple strings

A parsing template can parse multiple strings. This is effected by using the special pattern "," (comma) in the template – each comma is an instruction to the parser to move on to the next string. Other patterns and variables may be specified for each string parsed, as usual. The only time that multiple strings are available for parsing is in the ARG (or PARSE ARG) instruction; when an internal function or subroutine is invoked it may have several argument strings, and a comma is used to parse each in turn. Thus the template:

```
word1 rest1, string2, num
```

would put the first word of the first argument string into the variable WORD1, the rest of that string into REST1, and the next two strings into STRING2 and NUM. If insufficient strings were specified in the invocation, unused variables are set to null. Similarly, if only one string was available (as on the other PARSE variations) then any variables that follow a comma pattern are set to null.

If preferred, this use of commas in REXX may be thought of as a limited form of list notation.

SECTION 11: NUMBERS AND ARITHMETIC

REXX arithmetic attempts to carry out the usual operations (including addition, subtraction, multiplication, and division) in as "natural" a way as possible. What this really means is that the rules followed are those that are conventionally taught in schools and colleges. However, it was found that unfortunately the rules used vary considerably (indeed much more than generally appreciated) from person to person and from application to application and in ways that are not always predictable. The REXX arithmetic described here is therefore a compromise which (although not the simplest) should provide acceptable results in most applications.

Introduction

Numbers can be expressed in REXX very flexibly (leading and trailing blanks are permitted, exponential notation may be used) and follow conventional syntax. Some valid numbers are:

```
      12          /* A whole number            */
    '-76'         /* A signed whole number     */
      12.76       /* Some decimal places       */
  ' +  0.003 '    /* Blanks around the sign, etc. */
      17.         /* Equal to 17               */
       .5         /* Equal to 0.5              */
     4E9          /* Exponential notation      */
      0.73e-7     /* Exponential notation      */
```

(Exponential notation means that the number includes a power of ten following an "E" that indicates how the decimal point will be shifted. Thus 4E9 above is just a short way of writing 4000000000, and 0.73e-7 is short for 0.000000073.)

The **arithmetic operators** include addition ("+"), subtraction ("-"), multiplication ("*"), power ("**"), and division ("/"). There are also two further division operators: integer divide ("%") which divides and returns the integer part, and remainder ("//") which divides and returns the remainder. Prefix plus and prefix minus operators are also available.

When two numbers are combined by an operation, REXX uses a set of rules to define what the result will be (and how the result is to be represented as a character string). These rules are defined in the next section, but in summary:

- Results will be calculated with up to some maximum number of significant digits. For example, if a result required more than 9 digits it would normally be rounded to 9 digits. (The default is 9, but this may be altered with the NUMERIC instruction to give however many digits that you need.) For instance, the division of 2 by 3 would result in

0.666666667 (it would require an infinite number of digits for perfect accuracy).

- Except for the power and division operators, trailing zeros are preserved (this is in contrast to most electronic calculators, which remove all trailing zeros in the decimal part of results). So, for example:

```
2.40 + 2  =>  4.40
2.40 - 2  =>  0.40
2.40 * 2  =>  4.80
2.40 / 2  =>  1.2
```

This preservation of trailing zeros is desirable for most calculations (and especially financial calculations).

If necessary, trailing zeros may be easily removed with the STRIP function (see page 107), or by division by 1.

- A zero result is always expressed as the single digit '0'.

- Exponential form is used for a result depending on its value and the setting of NUMERIC DIGITS (the default is 9 digits). If the number of places needed before the decimal point exceeds this setting, or the number of places after the point exceeds twice the NUMERIC DIGITS setting, then the number will be expressed in exponential notation; thus

```
1e6 * 1e6  => 1E+12
                /* not 1000000000000 */
  1 / 3E10 => 3.33333333E-11
                /* not 0.0000000000333333333 */
```

Definition

This definition describes arithmetic in the REXX language.

Numbers

A *number* in REXX is a character string that includes one or more decimal digits, with an optional decimal point. The decimal point may be embedded in the digits, or may be prefixed or suffixed to them. The group of digits (and optional point) thus constructed may have leading or trailing blanks, and an optional sign ("+" or "-") which must come before any digits or decimal point. The sign may also have leading or trailing blanks. Thus:

```
sign    ::=  +  |  -
digit   ::=  0  |  1  |  2  |  3  |  4  |  5  |  6  |  7  |  8  |  9
digits  ::=  digit [digit]...
numeric ::=  digits . [digits]
             | [.] digits
number  ::=  [blank]... [sign [blank]...] numeric [blank]...
```

Note that a single period alone is not a valid number.

Precision

The maximum number of significant digits that can result from an arithmetic operation is controlled by the instruction:

```
NUMERIC DIGITS [expression];
```

The expression is evaluated and must result in a positive whole number. This defines the precision (number of significant digits) to which arithmetic calculations will be carried out; results will be rounded to that precision, if necessary.

If no expression is specified, then the default precision is used. The default precision is 9, that is, all implementations must support at least nine digits of precision. An implementation-dependent maximum (equal to or larger than 9) may apply: an attempt to exceed this will cause execution to terminate with an error message. Thus if an algorithm is defined to use more than 9 digits then if the NUMERIC DIGITS instruction succeeds then the computation will proceed and produce identical results to any other implementation.

Note that NUMERIC DIGITS may set values below the default of nine. Small values, however, should be used with care – the loss of precision and rounding thus requested will affect all REXX computations, including (for example) the computation of new values for the control variable in DO loops.

Arithmetic operators

REXX arithmetic is effected by the operators "+", "-", "*", "/", "%", "//", and "**" (add, subtract, multiply, divide, integer divide, remainder, and power) which all act upon two terms, together with the prefix plus and minus operators which both act on a single term. This section describes the way in which these operations are carried out.

Before every arithmetic operation, the term or terms being operated upon have leading zeros removed (noting the position of any decimal point, and leaving just one zero if all the digits in the number are zeros) and are then truncated to DIGITS+1 significant digits[39] (if necessary) before being used in the computation. The operation is then carried out under up to double that precision, as described under the individual operations below. When the operation is completed, the result is rounded if necessary to the precision specified by the NUMERIC DIGITS instruction.

Rounding is done in the "traditional" manner, in that the extra (guard) digit is inspected and values of 5 through 9 are rounded up, and values of 0 through 4 are rounded down.[40]

A conventional zero is supplied preceding a decimal point if otherwise there would be no digit before it. Trailing zeros are retained for addition, subtraction, and multiplication, according to the rules given below, except that a result of zero is always expressed as the single character '0'. For division, insignificant trailing zeros are removed after rounding.

The FORMAT built-in function is defined (see page 96) to allow a number to be represented in a particular format if the standard result provided by REXX does not meet requirements.

Arithmetic operation rules – basic operators

The basic operators (addition, subtraction, multiplication, and division) operate on numbers as follows:

Addition and subtraction

> If either number is zero then the other number, rounded to NUMERIC DIGITS digits if necessary, is used as the result (with sign adjustment as appropriate). Otherwise, the two numbers are extended on the right and left as necessary up to a total maximum of DIGITS+1 digits[41] and are then added or subtracted as appropriate. For example:

---

[39] That is, to the precision set by the NUMERIC DIGITS instruction, plus one extra "guard" digit.

[40] Even/odd rounding would require the ability to calculate to arbitrary precision (that is, to a precision not governed by the setting of NUMERIC DIGITS) at any time and is therefore not the mechanism defined for REXX.

[41] The number with smaller absolute value may therefore lose some or all of its digits

```
xxxx.xxx + yy.yyyyy
```

becomes:

```
   xxxx.xxx00
+  00yy.yyyyy
   ──────────
   zzzz.zzzzz
```

The result is then rounded to NUMERIC DIGITS digits if necessary, taking into account any extra (carry) digit on the left after an addition, but otherwise counting from the position corresponding to the most significant digit of the terms being added or subtracted. Finally, any insignificant leading zeros are removed.

The *prefix operators* are evaluated using the same rules; the operations "+number" and "-number" are calculated as "0+number" and "0-number", respectively.

Multiplication

The numbers are multiplied together ("long multiplication") resulting in a number which may be as long as the sum of the lengths of the two operands. For example:

```
xxx.xxx * yy.yyyyy
```

becomes:

```
zzzzz.zzzzzzzz
```

and the result is then rounded to the number of digits set by the NUMERIC DIGITS instruction, counting from the first significant digit of the result.

Division

For the division:

```
yyy / xxxxx
```

the following steps are taken: First the number "yyy" is extended with zeros on the right until it is larger than the number "xxxxx" (with note being taken of the change in the power of ten that this implies). Thus in this example, "yyy" might become "yyy00". Traditional long division then takes place, which can be written:

```
           zzzz
        ─────────
xxxxx ) yyy00
```

The length of the result ("zzzz") is such that the rightmost "z" will be at least as far right as the rightmost digit of the (extended) "y" number

---

on the right. In the example, the number yy.yyyyy would have three digits truncated if NUMERIC DIGITS 5 were in effect.

in the example. During the division, the "y" number will be extended
further as necessary, and the "z" number (which will not include any
leading zeros) may increase up to DIGITS+1 digits, at which point the
division stops and the result is rounded. Following completion of the
division (and rounding if necessary), insignificant trailing zeros are
removed.

Examples:

```
/* With NUMERIC DIGITS 5 */
12+7.00       ==    19.00
1.3-1.07      ==    0.23
1.3-2.07      ==    -0.77
1.20*3        ==    3.60
7*3           ==    21
0.9*0.8       ==    0.72
1/3           ==    0.33333
2/3           ==    0.66667
5/2           ==    2.5
1/10          ==    0.1
12/12         ==    1
8.0/2         ==    4
```

Note: With all the basic operators, the position of the decimal point in the
terms being operated upon is arbitrary. The operations may be carried out
as integer operations with the exponent being calculated and applied after-
wards. Therefore the significant digits of a result are not in any way
dependent on the position of the decimal point in either of the terms involved
in the operation.

Arithmetic operation rules – additional operators

The operation rules for the power ("$**$"), integer divide ("%"), and remainder
("//") operators are as follows:

Power

> The "$**$" (power) operator raises a number to a whole number power,
> which may be positive or negative.[42] If negative, the absolute value of
> the power is used, and then the result is inverted (divided into 1). For
> calculating the power, the number is effectively multiplied by itself for
> the number of times expressed by the power, and finally trailing zeros
> are removed (as though the result were divided by one).
>
> In practice (see note below for the reasons), the power is calculated by
> the process of left-to-right binary reduction. For "x**n": "n" is converted
> to binary, and a temporary accumulator is set to 1. If "n" has the value

---

[42] The second term in the operation must be a whole number and is therefore rounded
to DIGITS digits (if necessary), as described on page 137.

0 then the initial calculation is complete. Otherwise each bit (starting at the first non-zero bit) is inspected from left to right. If the current bit is 1 then the accumulator is multiplied by "x". If all bits have now been inspected then the initial calculation is complete, otherwise the accumulator is squared and the next bit is inspected for multiplication. When the initial calculation is complete, the temporary result is divided into 1 if the power was negative.

The multiplications and division are done under the normal arithmetic operation rules, detailed above, using a precision of DIGITS+L+1 digits. Here, L is the length in digits of the integer part of the whole number n (*i.e.*, excluding any decimal part, as though the built-in function TRUNC(n) had been used). Finally, the result is rounded to NUMERIC DIGITS digits, if necessary, and insignificant trailing zeros are removed.

Integer division

The "%" (integer divide) operator divides two numbers and returns the integer part of the result. The result returned is defined to be that which would result from repeatedly subtracting the divisor from the dividend while the dividend is larger than the divisor. During this subtraction, the absolute values of both the dividend and the divisor are used: the sign of the final result is the same as that which would result if normal division were used.

The result returned will have no fractional part (that is, no decimal point or zeros following it). If the result cannot be expressed as a whole number, the operation is in error and will fail – that is, the result must not have more digits than the current setting of NUMERIC DIGITS. For example, 10000000000%3 requires 10 digits for the result (3333333333) and would therefore fail if NUMERIC DIGITS 9 were in effect.

Remainder

The "//" (remainder) operator will return the remainder from integer division, and is defined as being the residue of the dividend after the operation of calculating integer division as just described. The sign of the remainder, if non-zero, is the same as that of the original dividend.

This operation will fail under the same conditions as integer division (that is, if integer division on the same two terms would fail, the remainder cannot be calculated).

Examples:

```
/* Again with NUMERIC DIGITS 5 */
2**3          ==   8
2**-3         ==   0.125
1.7**8        ==   69.758
2%3           ==   0
2.1//3        ==   2.1
10%3          ==   3
10//3         ==   1
-10//3        ==   -1
10.2//1       ==   0.2
10//0.3       ==   0.1
3.6//1.3      ==   1.0
```

Notes:

1. A particular algorithm for calculating powers is described, since it is efficient (though not optimal) and considerably reduces the number of actual multiplications performed. It therefore gives better performance than the simpler definition of repeated multiplication. Since results could possibly differ from those of repeated multiplication, the algorithm must be defined here so that different implementations will give identical results for the same operation on the same values. Other algorithms for this (and other) operations may always be used, so long as they give identical results to those described here.

2. The integer divide and remainder operators are defined so that they may be calculated as a by-product of the standard division operation (described above). The division process is ended as soon as the integer result is available; the residue of the dividend is the remainder.

Numeric comparisons

Any of the comparative operators (see page 26) may be used for comparing numeric strings. However, the strict comparisons (for example, "==" and ">>") are not numeric comparative operators and should not normally be used for comparing numbers, since leading and trailing blanks (and leading zeros) are significant for these operators.

Numeric comparison is effected by subtracting the two numbers (calculating the difference) and then comparing the result with '0' – that is, the operation

```
A ? B
```

where "?" is any numeric comparative operator, is identical to:

```
(A - B) ? '0'
```

It is therefore the *difference* between two numbers, when subtracted under REXX subtraction rules, that determines their equality.

Comparison of two numbers is affected by a quantity called *fuzz*, that controls the amount by which two numbers may differ before being considered equal for the purpose of comparison. The fuzz value is set by the instruction:

```
NUMERIC FUZZ [expression];
```

Here the expression must result in a whole number that is zero or positive. The default is 0.

The effect of NUMERIC FUZZ is to temporarily reduce the value of NUMERIC DIGITS by the NUMERIC FUZZ value for each numeric comparison – that is, the numbers are subtracted under a precision of DIGITS-FUZZ digits during the comparison. Clearly the NUMERIC FUZZ setting must be less than the setting of NUMERIC DIGITS.

Thus if DIGITS = 9, and FUZZ = 1, then the comparison will be carried out to 8 significant digits, just as though "NUMERIC DIGITS 8" had been put in effect for the duration of the operation.

Example:

```
numeric digits 5
numeric fuzz 0
say  4.9999 = 5      /* would display: 0 */
say  4.9999 < 5      /* would display: 1 */

numeric fuzz 1
say  4.9999 = 5      /* would display: 1 */
say  4.9999 < 5      /* would display: 0 */
```

An implementation-dependent maximum value for NUMERIC FUZZ (which could be 0) may apply: an attempt to exceed this will cause execution to terminate with an error message. Thus if an algorithm is defined to require a non-zero value of NUMERIC FUZZ then if the NUMERIC FUZZ instruction succeeds then the computation will proceed and produce identical results to any other implementation.

Exponential notation

The definition of numbers above (on page 129) describes "pure" numbers, in the sense that the character strings that describe numbers can be very long.

Examples:

```
say  10000000000 * 10000000000
/* would display: 100000000000000000000 */

say  .00000000001 * .00000000001
/* would display: 0.0000000000000000000001 */
```

For both large and small numbers some form of exponential notation is useful, both to make such long numbers more readable and to make execution possible in extreme cases. In addition, exponential notation is used whenever the "pure" form would give misleading information. For example:

```
numeric digits 5
say 54321*54321
```

would display "2950800000" if long form were to be used. This is clearly misleading, and so REXX would express the result in exponential notation, in this case "2.9508E+9".

The definition of *numbers* (see above) is therefore extended by replacing the description of *numeric* by the following:

```
mantissa ::=  digits . [digits]
            | [.] digits
numeric  ::=  mantissa [E [sign] digits]
```

In other words, the numeric part of a number may be followed by an "E" (indicating an exponential part), an optional sign, and an integer following the "E" (or sign) that represents a power of ten that is to be applied. The "E" may be in upper or lower case. Note that no blanks are permitted within this numeric part of a number.

Examples:

```
12E11   =  1200000000000
12E-5   =  0.00012
 12e4   =  120000
```

All valid numbers may be used as data for arithmetic. The results of calculations will be returned in exponential form depending on the setting of NUMERIC DIGITS. If the number of places needed before the decimal point exceeds NUMERIC DIGITS, or if the number of places after the point exceeds twice NUMERIC DIGITS, then exponential form will be used. The exponential form generated by REXX always has a sign following the "E" in order to improve readability. If the exponent is 0 then the exponential part is omitted – that is, an exponential part of "E+0" will never be generated.

If the default format for a number is not satisfactory for a particular application, then the FORMAT function may be used to control its format. Using this, numbers may be explicitly converted to exponential form or even forced to be returned in "pure" form. See page 96.

Different exponential notations may be selected with the NUMERIC FORM instruction. This instruction allows the selection of either scientific or engineering notation – see page 60. Scientific notation adjusts the power of ten so there is a single non-zero digit to the left of the decimal point. Engineering notation causes powers of ten to be expressed as a multiple of 3 – the integer part may therefore range from 1 through 999.

Examples:

```
numeric form scientific
say 123.45 * 1e11
/* would display: 1.2345E+13 */

numeric form engineering
say 123.45  * 1e11
/* would display: 12.345E+12 */
```

The default exponential notation is scientific.

Whole numbers

Within the set of numbers understood by REXX it is useful to distinguish the subset defined as *whole numbers*. A *whole number* in REXX is a number that has a decimal part which is all zeros (or that has no decimal part). In addition, it must be possible to express its integer part simply as digits within the precision set by the NUMERIC DIGITS instruction. (Larger numbers would be expressed by REXX in exponential notation, after rounding, and hence could no longer be safely described or used as "whole numbers".)

Numbers used directly by REXX

As discussed above, the result of any arithmetic operation is rounded (if necessary) according to the setting of NUMERIC DIGITS. Similarly, when a number (which has not necessarily been involved in an arithmetic operation) is used directly by REXX then the same rounding is also applied, just as though the operation of adding the number to 0 had been carried out.

In the following cases, the number used must be a whole number and an implementation restriction on the largest number that can be used may apply:

> positional patterns in parsing templates (including variable positional patterns)
> the power value (right hand operand) of the power operator
> the values of *exprr* and *exprf* in the DO instruction
> the values given for DIGITS or FUZZ in the NUMERIC instruction
> any number used in the *tracesetting* in the TRACE instruction.

Implementation minimum: A minimum length of 9 digits must be supported for these uses of whole numbers by a REXX language processor.

Implementation independence

The REXX arithmetic rules are defined in detail, so that when a given program is run the results of all computations are sufficiently defined that the same answer will result for all correct implementations. Differences due to the underlying machine architecture will not affect computations.

This contrasts with most other programming languages, where the result obtained may depend on the implementation because the precision and algorithms used by the language processor are defined by the implementation rather than by the language.

Errors

Two kinds of errors may occur during arithmetic:

- Overflow/Underflow

   This error will occur if the exponential part of a result would exceed the range that may be handled by the language processor, when the result is formatted according to the current settings of NUMERIC DIGITS and NUMERIC FORM. The language defines a minimum capability for the exponential part, namely exponents whose absolute value is at least as large as the largest number that can be expressed as an exact integer in default precision. Thus, since the default precision is 9, implementations must support exponents in the range -999999999 through 999999999.

- Insufficient storage

   Storage is needed for calculations and intermediate results, and on occasion an arithmetic operation may fail due to lack of storage. This is considered a terminating error as usual, rather than an arithmetical error.

SECTION 12:   INPUT AND OUTPUT STREAMS

The REXX language defines only simple, character oriented, forms of input and output. In general, communication to or from the user is in the form of a stream of characters. These streams may be manipulated either character-by-character or line-by-line. In addition to these character streams, a mechanism called the external data queue is defined for inter-program communication. This queue can only be accessed on a line-by-line basis.

In this discussion, input and output will be described as though communicating with a human user, but in many environments the character streams manipulated might have a variety of sources or destinations, such as files, serial interfaces, displays, or networks. The character streams may therefore be transient (for example, data sent or received over a serial interface) or they may be persistent (for example, files and objects). Housekeeping for the character streams (opening and closing files, for example) is not explicitly part of the language since in most environments these operations will be automatic; however, a function is provided for miscellaneous stream commands for those operating environments that require them.

It is assumed that there is one default input stream and one default output stream.[43] Simple instructions are provided to manipulate these default streams. The more general input and output routines allow the specification of a name for a stream, as well as other options. The name of the stream is necessarily implementation-dependent, but as illustrated below it is possible to write programs that use the input and output routines and yet are effectively independent of the underlying operating environment.

Error handling during input and output is necessarily heavily implementation-dependent; support for stream errors is provided by REXX in the form of a NOTREADY condition (that may be trapped by CALL ON or SIGNAL ON) and by a defined mechanism for determining the state of a named stream.

Components of input and output

The model of input and output for REXX consists of three logically distinct parts, namely one or more character input streams, one or more character output streams, and one external data queue. These are manipulated by the REXX instructions and built-in routines as follows:

Character input streams

A character input stream is a serial character stream conceptually generated by user interaction, or having the characteristics of a stream generated in that manner. Characters may be added to the end of some streams asynchronously, whereas other streams may be static or syn-

---

[43] These are often called the "standard input" and "standard output" streams.

chronous. A stream may be read directly as characters by the CHARIN function, or may be read as lines by the LINEIN function. The default input character stream will be read as lines by the PULL or PARSE PULL instructions if the external data queue is empty or is not implemented (PULL is the same as PARSE PULL except that upper case translation takes place). The PARSE LINEIN instruction may be used to read lines from the default input character stream regardless of the state of the external data queue, though normally the default input stream is read by using the PULL or PARSE PULL instructions.

The current *read position* in a stream is known to the REXX language processor (or, in some environments, is known to the system). The CHARS function will return the number of characters currently available in an input character stream from the read position through the end of the stream (including any line-end characters, if these are defined for the stream), and the LINES function similarly returns the number of complete lines available should the same stream be read as a series of lines.

Character output streams

Character output streams provide for output from a REXX program. A stream may be written with the CHAROUT routine (which usually provides complete control over the output stream), or may be written as lines using the LINEOUT routine. The default output stream may also be written as lines with the SAY instruction. The LINEOUT routine and the SAY instruction imply an appropriate line-end sequence at the end of each line. Depending on the stream being written other implementation-dependent modifications or formatting may apply, especially for line output.

The current *write position* in a stream, independent of the read position, is also known to the REXX language processor (or, in some environments, is known to the system). This is usually the end of the stream but for persistent files it may be possible to use this for sequential output from some arbitrary point.

The STREAM built-in function

The STREAM function is used to determine the state of an input or output stream, and may also be used to carry out implementation-defined stream operations (described by *stream commands*). This stream command mechanism is provided to allow for operating environments that have special requirements for the manipulation of certain input or output streams.

The external data queue

The external data queue is a queue of character strings that can only be accessed by line operations. It is external to REXX programs in that other programs may have access to the queue whenever REXX relinquishes control to some other program. Apart from the explicit REXX instructions described here, and in a single-process environment,[44] no detectable change to the queue will occur during the execution of a REXX program except when control leaves the program (for example when an external command or routine is called). The queue therefore forms a language-defined channel of communication between programs.

Data in the queue is arbitrary; no characters have any special meaning or effect. Lines may be removed from the queue using the PULL or PARSE PULL instructions (PULL is the same as PARSE PULL except that upper case translation takes place). When the queue is empty, these instructions will read lines from the default character input stream. This mechanism allows the external data queue to be used as a source for user input, provided that the user input is read as lines with these instructions.

Lines may be added to the head of the queue using the PUSH instruction, or to the tail of the queue using the QUEUE instruction. The QUEUED function returns the number of lines currently in the queue.

In many cases, a dialogue with a user will take place on a line-by-line basis. This kind of dialogue should be carried out with the SAY and PULL (or PARSE PULL) instructions. This technique considerably enhances the usability of many programs, as they may be converted to programmable dialogues by using the external data queue to provide the input normally entered by a user. PARSE LINEIN should only be used when it is necessary to bypass the external data queue.

When a dialogue is not on a line-by-line basis, the explicitly serial interfaces provided by the CHARIN and CHAROUT functions will be appropriate. These functions are especially important for input and output in the serial character stream environments provided by many operating environments.

Note: Input and output operations are necessarily implementation-dependent. Any implementation will therefore have to make decisions on the meaning of this description in a given environment. It is recognized that some implementations will not be able to follow this definition precisely. The input and output model here is intended to provide a framework which will allow for many environments and applications, but more complex situations may require routines and commands that are external to the REXX language. As usual, any such routines should be clearly identified in an implementation rather than being presented as part of (or an extension to) the language.

---

[44] That is, an environment in which (from the point of view of the program) queues are not shared by more than one process.

Errors During Input and Output

The REXX language offers implementations and programmers considerable flexibility in the handling of errors during input or output; this flexibility is necessary due to the wide variety of input and output streams that may be supported in different implementations.

When an error occurs during an input or output operation, the function being called will normally continue without interruption (with, for example, a non-zero count being returned by an output function). Depending on the nature of the operation the implementation has the option of raising the NOTREADY condition. The NOTREADY condition is similar to the ERROR and FAILURE conditions associated with commands in that it does not cause a terminating error if the condition is raised but is not trapped. Once NOTREADY has been raised, the following possibilities exist:

1. The NOTREADY condition is not being trapped: in this case execution continues without interruption; the NOTREADY condition remains in the OFF state.

2. The NOTREADY condition is being trapped by SIGNAL ON NOTREADY: in this case, the NOTREADY condition is raised, execution of the current clause ceases immediately, and the SIGNAL takes place as usual for condition traps.

3. The NOTREADY condition is being trapped by CALL ON NOTREADY: in this case the NOTREADY condition is raised, but execution of the current clause is not halted – the NOTREADY condition is put into the delayed state, and execution continues until the end of the current clause. While execution continues, input functions that refer to the same stream may return the null string, and output functions may return an appropriate count, depending on the form and timing of the error. At the end of the current clause, the CALL takes place as usual for condition traps.

4. The NOTREADY condition is being trapped (by CALL ON NOTREADY) but is already in the DELAY state (due to NOTREADY already having been raised): in this case execution continues, as in the first case, and the NOTREADY condition remains in the DELAY state.

Once the NOTREADY condition has been raised and is in DELAY state, the CONDITION function will return (for a "Description" invocation) the name of the stream being processed when the stream error occurred.[45]

The STREAM function will then usually show that the state of the stream is ERROR or NOTREADY, and additional information on the state of the stream will normally be available via the implementation-dependent "Description" option of the STREAM function.

---

[45] If the stream is a default stream and has no defined name, then the null string may be returned in this case.

Examples of input and output

In most circumstances, communication with a user running a REXX program
will be via the default input and output streams. For a question and answer
dialogue, the recommended technique is to use the SAY and PULL
instructions (using PARSE PULL if case sensitive input is required).
Examples of this have been given earlier, on pages 4 and 67.

More generally, though, it is necessary to write to or read from streams other
than the default. For example, to copy the contents of one file to another one
might use the following program:

FILECOPY

```
/* This routine copies the stream or file named by  */
/* the first argument to the stream or file named   */
/* by the second, as lines.                         */
parse arg inputname, outputname

do while lines(inputname)>0
  call lineout outputname, linein(inputname)
  end
```

While there are still some lines remaining in the named input stream, a line
is read and is then immediately written out to the named output stream. It
is easy to modify this program so that it filters the lines in some way before
they are written. Note that this program has no dependency on the form of
the names of the streams, which are likely to be implementation-dependent.

To illustrate how character and line operations might be mixed in a communications program, consider this example in which a character stream is
converted into lines:

COLLECTOR

```
/* This routine collects characters from the stream */
/* named by the first argument until a line is       */
/* complete, and then places the line on the         */
/* external data queue.                              */
/* The second argument is the single character that */
/* identifies the end of a line.                     */
parse arg inputname, lineendchar

buffer=''       /* zero-length character accumulator */
do forever
  nextchar=charin(inputname)
  if nextchar=lineendchar then leave
  buffer=buffer||nextchar              /* add to buffer */
  end
queue buffer /* place it on the external data queue */
```

Here each line is built up in a variable called BUFFER. When the line is complete (for example, if the stream comes from a user this might be when the RETURN or ENTER key is pressed) the loop is ended and the contents of BUFFER are placed on the external data queue. The program then ends.

Summary of the input and output instructions and functions:

CHARIN   Reads one or more characters from a character input stream. A start position may be specified for persistent streams. (Function, see page 86.)

CHAROUT   Writes zero or more characters to a character output stream. A start position may be specified for persistent streams. (Function, see page 87.)

CHARS   Returns the number of characters currently remaining in a character input stream. (Function, see page 88.)

LINEIN   Reads one line from a character input stream. A line number may be specified for persistent streams. (Function, see page 99.)

LINEOUT   Writes one line to a character output stream. A line number may be specified for persistent streams. (Function, see page 100.)

LINES   Returns the number of complete lines currently remaining in a character input stream. (Function, see page 101.)

PARSE LINEIN   Reads one line from the default character input stream. (Instruction, see page 62.)

PARSE PULL   Reads one line from the external data queue. If the queue is empty it reads a line from the default character input stream instead. (Instruction, see page 63.)

PULL   The same as PARSE PULL except that the string read is translated to upper case. (Instruction, see page 67.)

PUSH   Writes one line to the head of the external data queue, as in a stack. (Instruction, see page 68.)

QUEUE   Writes one line to the tail of the external data queue. (Instruction, see page 69.)

QUEUED   Returns the number of lines currently available in the external data queue. (Function, see page 103.)

SAY   Writes one line to the default character output stream. (Instruction, see page 70.)

STREAM   Returns a string describing the state of, or the result of an operation upon, a named character stream. (Function, see page 105.)

SECTION 13:   CONDITIONS AND CONDITION TRAPS

The flow of execution in a REXX program is normally explicitly determined by the instructions in the program. Under certain conditions, however, the explicit flow may be modified by *condition traps*.

Condition traps are turned on or off using the ON or OFF sub-keywords of the CALL and SIGNAL instructions:

$$\begin{Bmatrix} \text{CALL} \\ \text{SIGNAL} \end{Bmatrix} \begin{Bmatrix} \text{ON } condition \text{ [NAME } trapname \text{]} \\ \text{OFF } condition \end{Bmatrix} ;$$

where *condition* and *trapname* are single symbols which are taken as constants.

Following one of these instructions, a condition trap is set to be either ON (enabled) or OFF (disabled). The initial setting for all condition traps is OFF.

If a condition trap is enabled, then if the specified *condition* occurs, control will pass to the routine or label *trapname*. CALL or SIGNAL will be used, depending on whether the most recent trap for the condition was set ON using CALL ON or SIGNAL ON respectively.

The specified *condition* must be one of the following:

ERROR   raised if a command indicates an error condition upon return (see page 37). It is also raised if any command indicates failure and neither CALL ON FAILURE nor SIGNAL ON FAILURE are active. The condition is raised at the end of the clause that invoked the command, but will be ignored if the ERROR condition trap is already in the delayed state (see below).

FAILURE   raised if a command indicates a failure condition upon return (see page 37). The condition is raised at the end of the clause that invoked the command, but will be ignored if the FAILURE condition trap is already in the delayed state (see below).

HALT   raised if an external attempt is made to interrupt and terminate the execution of the program. The condition is normally raised at the end of the clause that was being executed when the external interruption took place.

NOVALUE   raised if a symbol (other than a constant symbol) is used as

                •   a term in an expression,

- the name following the VAR sub-keyword of a PARSE instruction,
- a variable reference in a parsing template, a PROCEDURE instruction, or a DROP instruction,

but does not have an assigned value. The NOVALUE condition may only be specified for SIGNAL ON (that is, CALL ON NOVALUE is not allowed).

NOTREADY raised when an error occurs during an input or output operation (see page 142). As for ERROR and FAILURE, the condition will be ignored if the NOTREADY condition trap is already in the delayed state (see below).

SYNTAX raised if any language processing error is detected while the programming is running. This includes all kinds of processing errors, including true syntax errors and "run time" errors (such as attempting an arithmetic operation on non-numeric terms). The SYNTAX condition may only be specified for SIGNAL ON (that is, CALL ON SYNTAX is not allowed).

Any ON or OFF reference to a condition trap will replace the previous state (ON, OFF, or DELAY, and any trap name) of that condition trap. Thus a CALL ON HALT would replace any current SIGNAL ON HALT (and *vice versa*), a CALL ON or SIGNAL ON with a new trap name would replace any previous trap name, any OFF reference will disable the trap for either CALL or SIGNAL, and so on.

Action taken when a condition is not trapped

When a condition trap is currently disabled (OFF) and the specified condition occurs, then the default action taken depends on the condition:

- For HALT and SYNTAX, the execution of the program is ended, and the condition is usually indicated by a message describing the nature of the event that occurred (see page 157).

- For all other conditions, the condition is ignored and its state remains OFF.

Action taken when a condition is trapped

When a condition trap is currently enabled (ON) and the specified condition occurs, then instead of the usual flow of control a "CALL *trapname*" or "SIGNAL *trapname*" is executed automatically. The trap name may be specified following the NAME sub-keyword of the CALL ON or SIGNAL ON instruction that enabled the condition trap. If no explicit trap name was given, then the name of the condition itself will be used as the trap name.

For example, the instruction

```
call on error
```

would enable the condition trap for the ERROR condition. If the condition occurred, then a call to the routine identified by the name ERROR would be made. If the instruction were

```
call on error   name commanderror
```

then the trap would be enabled and the routine COMMANDERROR would be called if the condition occurred.

The sequence of events, once a condition has been trapped, varies depending on whether a SIGNAL or CALL is to be made:

- If the action taken is a SIGNAL, then execution of the current instruction ceases immediately, the condition is disabled (set to OFF), and the SIGNAL takes place in exactly the same way as usual (see page 72).

  If any new occurrence of the condition is to be trapped, a new CALL ON or SIGNAL ON instruction for the condition is required to re-enable it once the label is reached. For example, if SIGNAL ON SYNTAX is enabled when a SYNTAX condition occurs, then if the SIGNAL ON SYNTAX label name is not found a normal syntax error termination will occur.

- If the action taken is a CALL (which can only take place at a clause boundary), then the "CALL *trapname*" is made in the usual way (see page 43) except that the special variable RESULT is not affected by the call. If the routine should RETURN any data, then the returned character string is ignored.

  Immediately the condition is raised, and before the CALL is made, the condition trap is put into a *delayed* state. This state persists until the RETURN from the CALL, or until an explicit CALL (or SIGNAL) ON (or OFF) is made for the condition. The delayed state prevents a premature condition trap at the start of a routine called to process a condition trap. When a condition trap is in the delayed state it remains enabled, but if the condition is raised again it is either ignored (for ERROR, FAILURE, or NOTREADY) or (for the other conditions) any action to be taken (including the updating of the condition information) will be delayed until one of the following events:

1.   A CALL ON or SIGNAL ON, for the delayed condition, is executed. In this case a CALL or SIGNAL will take place immediately after the new CALL ON or SIGNAL ON instruction has been executed.

2.   A CALL OFF or SIGNAL OFF, for the delayed condition, is executed. In this case the condition trap is disabled and the default action (see above) for the condition will occur at the end of the CALL OFF or SIGNAL OFF instruction.

3.   A RETURN is made from the subroutine. In this case the condition trap is no longer delayed and the subroutine will be called again immediately.

On RETURN from the CALL, the original flow of execution is resumed (that is, is not affected by the CALL).

Notes:

1.   In all cases, the condition will be raised immediately upon detection of the condition, and if trapped by SIGNAL ON the current instruction will be terminated (if necessary). Therefore the instruction during which such an event occurs may be only partly executed (for example, if SYNTAX is raised during the evaluation of the expression in an assignment, the assignment will not take place).

Note that the CALL for ERROR, FAILURE, HALT, and NOTREADY traps (the conditions for which CALL ON is allowed) can only occur at clause boundaries. Since these conditions can arise during execution of an INTERPRET instruction, execution of the INTERPRET may be interrupted and later resumed if CALL ON was used. Similarly, other instructions may be temporarily interrupted by a CALL at a clause boundary.

2.   The state (ON, OFF, or DELAY, and any trap name) of each condition trap is saved on entry to a subroutine and is then restored on RETURN. This means that CALL ON, CALL OFF, SIGNAL ON, and SIGNAL OFF may be used in a subroutine without affecting the conditions set up by the caller. See the CALL instruction (page 43) for details of other information that is saved during a subroutine call.

3.   The state of condition traps is not affected when an external routine is invoked by a CALL, even if the external routine is a REXX program. On entry to any REXX program all condition traps have an initial setting of OFF.

4.   While user input is executed during interactive tracing, all condition traps are temporarily disabled (set OFF). This prevents any unexpected transfer of control should (for example) the user accidentally use an uninitialized variable while SIGNAL ON NOVALUE is active. For the same reason, a syntax error during interactive tracing will not cause exit from the program, but is trapped specially and is then ignored after a message is given.

5.   Certain execution errors may be detected by the system interface either before execution of the program starts or after the program has ended. These errors cannot be trapped by SIGNAL ON SYNTAX, and are outside the scope of the language.

Condition Information

When any condition is trapped and causes a SIGNAL or CALL, it becomes the *current trapped condition* and certain *condition information* associated with it is recorded. This information may be inspected by using the built-in function CONDITION (see page 89).

The condition information includes the name of the current trapped condition, the name of the instruction executed as a result of the condition trap ('CALL' or 'SIGNAL'), the state of the condition, and a descriptive string. The descriptive string varies, depending on the condition trapped:

ERROR   The string which, when passed to the external environment as a command, was processed and resulted in the error condition.

FAILURE   The string which, when passed to the external environment as a command, was processed and resulted in the failure condition.

HALT   Any string associated with the halt request by the external environment. This may be the null string if no specific string was provided.

NOVALUE   The derived name of the variable whose attempted reference caused the NOVALUE condition.

NOTREADY   The name of the stream being manipulated when the error occurred and the NOTREADY condition was raised. If the stream was a default stream with no defined name then the null string may be returned.

SYNTAX   Any string associated with the error by the language processor. This may be the null string if no specific string was provided. Note that the special variables RC and SIGL provide information on the nature and position of the processing error.

The current condition information is replaced when control is passed to a label as the result of a condition trap (CALL ON or SIGNAL ON). Condition information is saved and restored across subroutine or function calls, including one due to a CALL ON trap. Therefore, a routine invoked due to CALL ON can access the appropriate condition information and any previous condition information will still be available after the routine returns.

The special variable RC

When an ERROR or FAILURE condition is trapped the special variable RC is set to the command return code, as usual, before control is transferred to the target label (whether by CALL or by SIGNAL).

Similarly, when a SYNTAX condition is trapped by SIGNAL ON SYNTAX, the special variable RC is set to the syntax error number before control is transferred to the target label.

The special variable SIGL

Following the execution of any jump due to a CALL or SIGNAL, the program line number of the instruction causing the jump is stored in the special variable SIGL. Where the jump is due to a condition trap, the line number assigned to SIGL is that of the last clause executed (at the current subroutine level) before the CALL or SIGNAL actually took place.

The setting of SIGL is especially useful after a SIGNAL ON SYNTAX trap (see above) when the number of the line in error can be used, for example, to control a text editor. Typically code following the SYNTAX label may PARSE SOURCE to find the source of the data, then invoke an editor to edit the source program, positioned at the line in error.[46]

Alternatively SIGL may be used to help determine the cause of an error (such as the occasional failure of a function call), using the following section of code (or something similar):

```
/* Standard handler for SIGNAL ON SYNTAX */
Syntax:
   say 'REXX error' rc 'in line' sigl':' errortext(rc)
   say sourceline(sigl)
   trace '?r'; nop
```

This code displays the error code, line number, and error message, then displays the line in error, and finally drops into interactive tracing to allow you to inspect the values of the variables used at the line in error (for example). This could be followed by instructions to place the user into an editor at the line in error, as just described.

---

[46] Depending upon the implementation, the program may have to be recompiled and/or re-invoked before any changes made in the editor can take effect.

SECTION 14:   INTERACTIVE TRACING

The REXX language includes a mechanism for interactively controlling the execution of a program. This interactive tracing mechanism is optional, in that not all implementations will include it, but implementations should remain consistent with it wherever appropriate.

Changing the TRACE setting to one with a prefix "?" (for example, "TRACE ?All", or using the TRACE built-in function) turns on interactive tracing, and also informs the user that tracing is now interactive. The language processor will then ignore further TRACE instructions in the program, and will pause after nearly all clauses that are traced (see below for exceptions). Once the processor has paused then three actions are possible:

1. **Entering a null line** (no blanks even) will make the language processor continue execution until the next pause for interactive input. Repeatedly entering a null line will therefore step from pause point to pause point. For "TRACE ?All", for example, this is equivalent to single-stepping through the program.

2. **Entering an equals sign ("=")** will make the language processor re-execute the clause last traced. If an IF clause is about to take the wrong branch, for example, you can change the value of the variable(s) on which it depends and then re-execute it.

    Once the clause has been re-executed, the processor will pause again. The equals sign may not have leading or trailing blanks.

3. **Anything else entered** will be treated as a string of one or more clauses to be interpreted immediately. They are executed by the same mechanism as the INTERPRET instruction, and the same rules apply (for example, DO...END constructs must be complete, *etc.*). If an instruction has a syntax error in it, a standard message will be displayed and you will be prompted for input again – the error will not be trapped by SIGNAL ON SYNTAX or cause exit from the program. Similarly all the other condition traps are temporarily disabled while the string is interpreted, to prevent unintentional transfer of control.

    During interpretation of the string, no tracing takes place, except that error return codes from commands are displayed. The special variable RC is not set by commands executed from the string.

    Once the string has been interpreted, the language processor pauses again for further interactive input unless a TRACE instruction was executed during the interpretation. In this latter case the processor will immediately alter the trace setting (if necessary) and then continue executing until the next pause point (if any). Hence to alter the trace setting (from "All" to "Results" for example) and then re-execute the instruction, you must use the built-in TRACE function (see page 110). For example, "CALL TRACE I" will ensure that the trace setting is "I" and allow re-execution of the clause after which the pause was made. Interactive tracing will be turned off only if a TRACE instruction uses a "?" prefix (or is "TRACE Off" or "TRACE").

The numeric form of TRACE setting may be used to allow sections of the program to be executed without pause for interactive input. "TRACE n", (*i.e.*, positive result) will allow execution to continue, with the next "n" pauses (when tracing is interactive) being skipped. "TRACE -n", (*i.e.*, negative result) will allow execution to continue without pause and with tracing inhibited for "n" clauses that would otherwise be traced.

The trace action selected by a TRACE instruction is saved and restored across subroutine calls. This means that if you are stepping through a program (say after using "TRACE ?Results") then enter a subroutine in which you have no interest, you can then enter "TRACE Off". No further instructions in the subroutine will be traced, but on return to the caller tracing will be restored.

Similarly, if you are interested only in a subroutine, you can put a "TRACE ?R" instruction at its start. Having traced the routine, the original state of tracing will be restored and hence (if tracing was off on entry to the subroutine) all tracing will be turned off until the next entry to the subroutine.

Interactive tracing is usefully controlled externally, so that it may be switched on without modifying the program. Under the VM/CMS operating system, for example, tracing may be switched on, without requiring modification to a program, by using the SET EXECTRAC ON command (which will turn the system tracing bit on or off). Tracing may be also turned on asynchronously, (*i.e.*, while a program is running) using the "ts" immediate command.

Since any instructions may be executed during interactive tracing you have considerable control over execution.

Examples:

say expr   will display the result of evaluating the expression.

name=expr   will alter the value of a variable.

trace off   (or just "TRACE") will turn off all tracing.

trace ?all
            will turn off interactive tracing but continue tracing all clauses.

trace L   will make the language processor pause at labels only. This is similar to the traditional "breakpoint" function, except that you do not have to know the exact name and spelling of the labels in the program.

exit   will terminate execution of the program.

```
do i=1 to 10; say stem.i; end;
```
        would display ten elements of the array "STEM.".

Exceptions: Some clauses may not be safely re-executed, and therefore a language processor would not pause after them even if they are traced. These are:

- Any repetitive DO clause, on the second or subsequent time around the loop.

- All END clauses (not a useful place to pause in any case).

- All THEN, ELSE, OTHERWISE, or null clauses.

- All RETURN and EXIT clauses.

- All SIGNAL and CALL clauses (but the processor can pause after the target label has been traced).

- Any clause that raises a condition which is trapped by a CALL ON or SIGNAL ON (that is, the pause will take place after the target label for the CALL or SIGNAL has been traced).

- Any clause that causes a syntax error. (These may be trapped by SIGNAL ON SYNTAX, but cannot be re-executed.)

SECTION 15:   RESERVED KEYWORDS AND LANGUAGE EXTENDIBILITY

The free syntax of REXX implies that the language must reserve a few symbols in certain contexts. These will always be *simple symbols* (see page 33) – other forms of symbol are never reserved.

Within particular instructions, some symbols may be reserved to separate the parts of the instruction: for example the sub-keyword WHILE in a DO instruction, or the keyword THEN (which acts as a clause terminator in this case) following an IF or WHEN clause.

Apart from these cases, only simple symbols that are the first token in a clause and that are not followed by a token that starts with an "=" or ":" are checked to see if they are instruction keywords – the symbols may be freely used elsewhere in clauses without being taken to be keywords.

Therefore keywords can only adversely affect the user when it is desired to execute a command with the same name (for example "QUEUE") as a REXX keyword. This is potentially a problem for any programmer whose REXX programs might be used for some time and in circumstances outside his or her control, and who wishes to make the programs absolutely "watertight". When this is required, a REXX program should be written with (at least) the first word in every command enclosed in quotes.

Example:

```
'ERASE' fn ft
```

This also has an advantage in that it is more efficient; and with this style, the SIGNAL ON NOVALUE condition trap may be used to assure the integrity of a program.

An alternative strategy is to precede such command strings with two adjacent quotes, which will have the effect of concatenating the null string on to the front.

Example:

```
''Erase fn ft
```

A third but perhaps more ugly option is to enclose the entire expression (or the first symbol) in parentheses.

Example:

```
(Erase fn ft)
```

Importantly, the choice of strategy (if it is to be done at all) is a personal one by the programmer, and is not imposed by the REXX language.

The possibility of identifying all REXX keywords by starting them with a unique character (for example ".") was most seriously considered, however this:

- does not solve the problem in the case of an addressed environment that supports commands starting with that character.

- destroys the natural look of the language that was one of the prime reasons for its design.

In addition to this, it was felt that the problem is rather less severe than that of changes to the commands invoked by the program: these are often far less controlled and may even have totally different effects in different locations and environments. The problem is also less severe than the problem of sub-keywords within instructions. Attempts to define a mechanism so that sub-keywords need not be reserved led to even less desirable properties.

SECTION 16:   SPECIAL VARIABLES

There are three *special variables* that may be set automatically during execution of a REXX program:

RC   is set to the return code from any executed command (including those submitted with the ADDRESS instruction). Following the trapping of the conditions ERROR or FAILURE it is also set to the command return code. When the SYNTAX condition is trapped, RC is set to the syntax error number (1-99). RC is unchanged when a NOVALUE or HALT condition is trapped.

Note: Commands executed manually while tracing interactively do not cause the value of RC to change.

RESULT is set by a RETURN instruction in a subroutine that has been called, if the RETURN instruction specifies an expression. If the RETURN instruction has no expression on it then RESULT is dropped (becomes uninitialized).

SIGL   contains the line number of the last instruction that caused a jump to a label (*i.e.*, any SIGNAL, CALL, internal function invocation, or trapped condition).

None of these variables has an initial value. They may be altered by the user, just like any other variable, but will continue to be set automatically by REXX when appropriate. The PROCEDURE and DROP instructions also affect these variables in their usual way.

Certain other information is available to a REXX program. This usually includes the name by which the program was invoked and the source of the program (which are available using the PARSE SOURCE instruction, see page 63). In addition, PARSE VERSION (see page 64) makes available the language version and date of the language processor that is running; and the built-in functions ADDRESS, DIGITS, FUZZ, FORM, and TRACE return other settings that affect the execution of a program.

SECTION 17:   ERROR NUMBERS AND MESSAGES

The error numbers produced by errors during execution of REXX programs are all in the range 1-99 (and this is the value placed in the variable RC when SIGNAL ON SYNTAX is trapped).

The recommended error numbers with their meaning and suggested messages are as follows. An implementation should normally use the recommended error number wherever possible, though the message itself may change as appropriate (for instance, to a language that is not English). The text of the error message is available using the ERRORTEXT built-in function (see page 95).

In general an error message will also include other information, such as a line number or more specific information describing where in the program the error occurred.

4 – Program interrupted

The system interrupted execution of a REXX program because of some error, or by user request.

Unless trapped by CALL ON HALT or SIGNAL ON HALT, this will make the language processor immediately cease execution with this message.

5 – Machine resources exhausted

While attempting to execute a REXX program, the language processor was unable to obtain the resources it needs to continue execution. (For example, it could not obtain the space needed for its work areas, variables, *etc.*)

6 – Unmatched "/*" or quote

A comment or literal string was started but never finished. This may be detected at the end of the program (or end of data in an INTERPRET instruction) for comments, or at the end of a line for strings.

7 – WHEN or OTHERWISE expected

Within a SELECT construct, at least one WHEN construct (and possibly an OTHERWISE clause) is expected. If any other instruction is found (or no WHEN construct is found before the OTHERWISE) then this message results.

This is commonly caused by forgetting the DO and END around the list of instructions following a WHEN. For example:

```
select
  when a=b then
    say "A Equals B"
    exit
  otherwise nop
  end
```

should be:

```
select
  when a=b then do
    say "A Equals B"
    exit
    end
  otherwise nop
  end
```

8 – *Unexpected THEN or ELSE*

A THEN or an ELSE has been found that does not match a corresponding IF (or WHEN) clause.

This error often occurs because of a missing END or DO...END in the THEN part of a complex IF...THEN...ELSE construction. For example:

```
if a=b then do
  say "Equals"
  exit
else
  say "Not equals"
```

should have an END immediately following the EXIT instruction.

9 – *Unexpected WHEN or OTHERWISE*

A WHEN or an OTHERWISE has been found outside of a SELECT construct. It may have been enclosed unintentionally in a DO...END construct by leaving off an END instruction; or an attempt may have been made to branch to it with a SIGNAL instruction (which cannot work as a SELECT is terminated by a SIGNAL).

10 – *Unexpected or unmatched END*

There are more ENDs in the program than DOs and SELECTs, or the ENDs are wrongly placed so they do not match the DOs and SELECTs.

Putting the name of the control variable on ENDs that close repetitive loops helps to avoid or locate this kind of error.

A common mistake that causes this error is attempting to jump into the middle of a loop using the SIGNAL instruction. Since the previous DO will not have been executed, the END is unexpected. Remember, too, that

SIGNAL deactivates any current loops, so it may not be used to jump from one place inside a loop to another.

This error will also be generated if an END immediately follows a THEN or an ELSE.

11 – *Control stack full*

An implementation limit of levels of nesting of control structures (DO...END, IF...THEN...ELSE, INTERPRET, *etc.*) has been exceeded (the message should state the actual restriction).

This could be due to a looping INTERPRET instruction, for example:

```
line='INTERPRET line'
interpret line
```

which would otherwise loop forever. Similarly a recursive subroutine or internal function that does not terminate correctly could loop forever.

12 – *Clause too long*

There may be an implementation restriction that limits the length of the internal or external representation of a clause – this message is generated if this limit is exceeded (the message should state the actual restriction size, for example: *"Clause > 1000 Characters"*).

13 – *Invalid character in program*

The program includes a character outside of a literal (quoted) string that is not a blank or one of the following:

```
A-Z, a-z, 0-9                        (Alphanumerics)
? ! . underscore                     (Name chars)
& * ( ) - + = ¬ \ | / ' " ; : < , > % (Specials)
```

The most common cause for this error is the use of accented and other language-specific characters in symbols when not permitted by the implementation.

14 – *Incomplete DO/SELECT/IF*

On reaching the end of the program (or end of the string in an INTER-PRET instruction), it has been detected that there is a DO or SELECT without a matching END, or an IF that is not followed by a THEN clause to execute.

Putting the name of the control variable on ENDs that close repetitive loops helps to avoid or locate this kind of error.

15 – Invalid hexadecimal or binary string

Hexadecimal strings may not have leading or trailing blanks, and may only have embedded blanks at byte boundaries. Only the digits 0-9 and the letters a-f and A-F are allowed. Similarly, binary strings may only have blanks added at the boundaries of groups of four binary digits, and only the digits 0 and 1 are allowed.

The error may also be caused by following a literal string by the one-character symbol "X" (for example the name of the variable X) when the string is not intended to be taken as a hexadecimal specification, or by the symbol "B" when the string is not intended to be taken as a binary specification. Use the explicit concatenation operator, "| |", in these situations to concatenate the string to the value of the symbol.

16 – Label not found

A SIGNAL instruction has been executed (or an event for which a trap was set has occurred), and the label specified cannot be found in the program.

The name of the label for which the search was made should be included in the message or in the error traceback.

17 – Unexpected PROCEDURE

A PROCEDURE instruction was encountered which was not the first instruction executed after a CALL or function invocation.

A possible cause of this is "dropping through" into an internal routine rather than invoking it properly.

18 – THEN expected

All IF clauses and WHEN clauses in REXX must be followed by a THEN clause. Some other clause was found when a THEN was expected.

19 – String or symbol expected

On the SIGNAL or CALL instructions a literal string or a symbol was expected but neither was found.

20 – Symbol expected

In the clauses CALL ON, END, ITERATE, LEAVE, NUMERIC, PARSE, and SIGNAL ON, a symbol can be expected. Either it was not present when required, or some other token was found.

Alternatively, DROP, and the EXPOSE option of PROCEDURE, expect a list of symbols or variable references. Some other token was found.

21 – Invalid data on end of clause

A clause such as SELECT or NOP is followed by some token other than a comment.

22 – Invalid character string

This error results if a literal string contains character codes that are not valid in a particular implementation. This might be because some characters are "impossible", or because the character set is extended in some way and certain character combinations are not allowed.

23 – Invalid data string

This error results if a data string (result of an expression, *etc.*) contains character codes that are not valid in a particular implementation. This might be because some characters are "impossible", or because the character set is extended in some way and certain character combinations are not allowed.

24 – Invalid TRACE request

The setting specified on a TRACE instruction starts with a character that does not match one of the valid TRACE settings (*i.e.*, A, C, E, F, I, L, N, O, or R).

25 – Invalid sub-keyword found

An unexpected token has been found in the position in an instruction where a particular sub-keyword was expected.

For example, in a NUMERIC instruction, the second token must be DIGITS, FUZZ, or FORM, and anything else is in error.

26 – Invalid whole number

One of the following did not evaluate to a whole number (or is greater than the implementation limit, for these uses):

> positional patterns in parsing templates (including variable positional patterns)
> the power value (right hand operand) of the power operator
> the values of *exprr* and *exprf* in the DO instruction
> the values given for DIGITS or FUZZ in the NUMERIC instruction
> any number used in the *tracesetting* in the TRACE instruction.

This error is also raised if the value is not permitted (for example, a negative repetition count in a DO instruction), or when the division performed during an integer divide (or remainder) operation does not result in a whole number.

27 – Invalid DO syntax

Some syntax error has been found in the DO instruction. This might be using BY, TO, or FOR twice, or using BY, TO, or FOR when there is no control variable specified, *etc.*

28 – Invalid LEAVE or ITERATE

A LEAVE or ITERATE instruction was encountered in an invalid position. Either no loop is active, or the name specified on the instruction does not match the control variable of any active loop. Note that since internal routine calls and the INTERPRET instruction protect DO loops, they become inactive. Therefore, for example, a LEAVE in a subroutine cannot affect a DO loop in the calling routine.

A common cause for this error message is attempting to use the SIGNAL instruction to transfer control within or into a loop. Since SIGNAL terminates all active loops, an ITERATE or LEAVE would then be in error.

29 – Environment name too long

The environment name specified by the ADDRESS instruction is longer than permitted for the system under which REXX is executing. The message should state the maximum permitted length.

30 – Name or string too long

This error results if there is an implementation limit on the length of a variable name or label name (or on the length of a literal string) and it is exceeded.

The limit exceeded should be included in the message, for example: *"Name or String > 100 characters"*.

31 – Name starts with number or "."

A value may not be assigned to a variable whose name starts with a numeric digit or a period (since if it were permitted one could re-define numeric constants).

33 – Invalid expression result

The result of an expression in an instruction was found to be invalid in the particular context in which it was used. This may be due to an illegal FUZZ or DIGITS value in a NUMERIC instruction (FUZZ may not become larger than DIGITS).

34 – Logical value not 0 or 1

The expression in an IF, WHEN, DO WHILE or DO UNTIL phrase must result in a '0' or a '1', as must any term operated on by a logical operator (that is, ¬ \ | & &&).

35 – Invalid expression

This is due to a grammatical error in an expression, such as ending it with an operator, or having two operators adjacent with nothing in between. It may also be due to an expression that is missing when one is required.

A common error is to include special characters (such as operators) in an intended character expression without enclosing them in quotes.

36 – Unmatched "(" in expression

This is due to not pairing parentheses correctly within an expression. There are more left parentheses than right parentheses.

37 – Unexpected "," or ")"

In an expression, either a comma has been found outside a function invocation, or there are too many right parentheses.

38 – Invalid template or pattern

Within a parsing template, a special character that is not allowed (for example, "%") has been found, or the syntax of a variable pattern is incorrect (*i.e.*, no symbol was found after a left parenthesis). This error may also be raised if the WITH sub-keyword is omitted in a PARSE VALUE instruction.

39 – Evaluation stack overflow

The expression is too complex to be evaluated by the language processor. There are too many nested parentheses, functions, and so on. (The message should state the actual restriction.)

40 – Incorrect call to routine

The specified built-in or external routine does exist, but it has been used incorrectly. Either invalid arguments were passed to the routine, or the program invoked was not compatible with the REXX language processor, or more than an implementation-limited number of arguments were passed to the routine.

41 – Bad arithmetic conversion

One of the terms involved in an arithmetic operation is not a valid number, or its exponent exceeds the implementation limit (often 9 digits).

42 – Arithmetic overflow/underflow

The result of an arithmetic operation requires an exponent that is outside the range supported by the implementation, perhaps greater than 999999999, or less than -999999999.

This can happen during evaluation of an expression (commonly an attempt to divide a number by 0), or possibly during the stepping of a DO loop control variable.

43 – Routine not found

A function has been invoked within an expression (or a subroutine has been invoked by CALL) but it cannot be found. No label with the specified name exists in the program, it is not the name of a built-in function, and the language processor has been unable to locate it externally. The name has probably been mis-typed, or it is possible that a symbol or literal string is adjacent to a "(" when it was meant to be separated by a blank or some other operator. This will be understood as a function invocation. For example:

```
3(4+5)   should be written   3*(4+5)
```

44 – Function did not return data

An external function has been invoked within an expression, but even though it appeared to end without error, it did not return data for use within the expression.

45 – No data specified on function RETURN

The program has been called as a function, but an attempt is being made (by RETURN;) to return without passing back any data.

Similarly, if an internal routine is called as a function then the RETURN instruction that ends it must specify an expression.

46 – Invalid variable reference

Within an ARG, DROP, PARSE, PULL, or PROCEDURE instruction, the syntax of a variable reference (a variable whose value is to be used, indicated by its name being enclosed in parentheses) is incorrect. The right parenthesis that should immediately follow the variable name is missing.

48 – Failure in system service

Some system service used by the REXX language processor (such as stream input or output, or manipulation of the external data queue) has failed to work correctly and hence normal execution cannot continue.

49 – Interpretation error

Implementations of the language will normally carry out internal self-consistency checks during execution. This message indicates that some kind of severe error has been detected within the language processor or execution process.

Appendix A: REXX Syntax Diagrams

This appendix collects together the syntax diagrams of the REXX instructions presented earlier in this book. They include general terms defined on the following pages:

expression Page 24.

instruction Page 31.

name   Pages 21 and 32-37.

pattern   Page 118.

string   Page 19.

symbol   Page 21.

template   Page 118.

Other terms specific to individual instructions are explained in the section describing that instruction.

Assignment:

---
symbol = *expression* ;

Command:

---
expression ;

Keyword Instructions:

ADDRESS $\begin{bmatrix} environment & [exprc] \\ [\text{VALUE}] & exprv \end{bmatrix}$;

where *environment* is a symbol or literal string, which is taken as a constant, and *exprc* and *exprv* are *expressions*.

ARG [*template*] ;

where *template* is a list of symbols separated by blanks and/or patterns.

CALL $\begin{Bmatrix} name \ [expression] \ [\ , \ [expression]] \ ... \\ \text{ON } condition \ [\text{NAME } trapname] \\ \text{OFF } condition \end{Bmatrix}$;

where *name* is a symbol or literal string which is taken as a constant, and *condition* and *trapname* are single symbols which are taken as constants.

DO [*repetitor*] [*conditional*] ;
   [*instructionlist*]
   END [*symbol*] ;

where *repetitor* is one of

   name = *expri* [TO *exprt*] [BY *exprb*] [FOR *exprf*]
   exprr
   FOREVER

and *conditional* is either of

   WHILE *exprw*
   UNTIL *expru*

and *instructionlist* is

   any sequence of *instructions*

and *expri*, *exprt*, *exprb*, *exprf*, *exprr*, *exprw*, and *expru* are *expressions*.

DROP *variablelist* ;

where *variablelist* is one or more symbols (optionally enclosed in parentheses) separated by blanks.

EXIT [*expression*] ;

IF *expression* [;] THEN [;] *instruction* [ELSE [;] *instruction*]

INTERPRET *expression* ;

ITERATE [*name*] ;

where *name* is a symbol, taken as a constant.

LEAVE [*name*] ;

where *name* is a symbol, taken as a constant.

NOP;

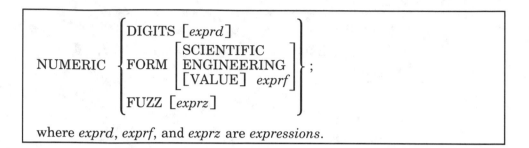

NUMERIC {
  DIGITS [*exprd*]
  FORM [SCIENTIFIC / ENGINEERING / [VALUE] *exprf*]
  FUZZ [*exprz*]
} ;

where *exprd*, *exprf*, and *exprz* are *expressions*.

OPTIONS *expression* ;

PARSE [UPPER] {
  ARG
  LINEIN
  PULL
  SOURCE
  VALUE [*expression*] WITH
  VAR *name*
  VERSION
} [*template*] ;

where *template* is a list of symbols separated by blanks and/or patterns.

PROCEDURE [EXPOSE *variablelist*] ;

where *variablelist* is one or more symbols (optionally enclosed in parentheses) separated by blanks.

PULL [*template*] ;

where *template* is a list of symbols separated by blanks and/or patterns.

PUSH [*expression*] ;

QUEUE [*expression*] ;

RETURN [*expression*] ;

SAY [*expression*] ;

SELECT ; *whenlist* [OTHERWISE [;] [*instructionlist*]] END ;

where *whenlist* is:

one or more *whenconstruct*s

and *whenconstruct* is:

WHEN *expression* [;] THEN [;] *instruction*

and *instructionlist* is:

any sequence of *instructions*

SIGNAL $\begin{cases} labelname \\ [VALUE]\ expression \\ ON\ condition\ [NAME\ trapname] \\ OFF\ condition \end{cases}$;

where *labelname* is a symbol or literal string which is taken as a constant, and *condition* and *trapname* are single symbols which are taken as constants.

TRACE $\begin{bmatrix} tracesetting \\ [VALUE]\ expression \end{bmatrix}$;

where *tracesetting* is a symbol or literal string which is taken as a constant.

Appendix B: A Sample REXX Program

This appendix includes a short program, called QT, which is an example of a "real" REXX program. The programs included elsewhere in this book have been contrived to illustrate specific points. By contrast, QT is a simple but heavily used tool that genuinely improves the human factors of computer systems. People frequently wish to know the time of day, and QT presents this information in a natural way.

The style used for this example is the same as that used throughout the book, with all symbols except labels being written in lower case. Other REXX programming styles are possible, of course; for another successful style, see O'Hara and Gomberg's *Modern Programming Using REXX*.

QT has the distinction of being one of the first REXX programs ever written. It has been changed, however, since it was first written – early versions of REXX did not allow multiple argument strings.

QT – Query Time

```
/*-----------------------------------------------------------*/
/* QT: This program displays the time in natural English. */
/* Two argument strings may be supplied.  If "?" is given */
/* as the first argument then the program displays a      */
/* description of itself.  If a second argument is given  */
/* it is used as a test value to check that the program   */
/* works.  This second value must be a time in the format */
/* HH:MM:SS; it does not have its syntax checked.         */
/*-----------------------------------------------------------*/

/*--------- First process the argument strings -----------*/
parse arg parm, testtime .     /* get the argument strings */
select
  when parm='?' then call tell           /* say what we do */
  when parm=''  then nop         /* OK (no first argument) */
  otherwise
    say 'Only "?" is a valid argument to QT.  The argument'
    say 'that you supplied ("'parm'") has been ignored.'
    call tell  /* usually helpful to describe the program */
  end

if testtime='' then now=time()   /* default; use time now */
                else now=testtime   /* caller's test value */

/*--------- Now start processing in earnest --------------*/
/* Nearness phrases - use compound variable, as example   */
near.0=''                                      /* exact */
near.1=' just gone';  near.2=' just after'      /* after */
near.3=' nearly';     near.4=' almost'         /* before */

/* Extract the hours, minutes, and seconds from the time. */
parse var now hour':'min':'sec

if sec>29 then min=min+1              /* round up minutes */
mod=min//5           /* where we are in 5 minute bracket */
out="It's"near.mod       /* start building the result */
if min>32 then hour=hour+1        /* we are TO the hour... */
min=min+2      /* shift minutes to straddle 5-minute point */

/* Now special-case the result for Noon and Midnight      */
if hour//12=0 & min//60<=4 then do
  if hour=12 then say out 'Noon.'
            else say out 'Midnight.'
  exit; end                        /* we are finished here */
```

continued…

```
min=min-(min//5)                        /* find nearest 5 mins */
if hour>12
  then hour=hour-12                 /* get rid of 24-hour clock */
  else
    if hour=0 then hour=12       /* .. and allow for midnight */

/* Determine the phrase to use for each 5-minute segment  */
select
  when min= 0 then nop                /* add "o'clock" later */
  when min=60 then min=0                              /* ditto */
  when min= 5 then out=out 'five past'
  when min=10 then out=out 'ten past'
  when min=15 then out=out 'a quarter past'
  when min=20 then out=out 'twenty past'
  when min=25 then out=out 'twenty-five past'
  when min=30 then out=out 'half past'
  when min=35 then out=out 'twenty-five to'
  when min=40 then out=out 'twenty to'
  when min=45 then out=out 'a quarter to'
  when min=50 then out=out 'ten to'
  when min=55 then out=out 'five to'
  end

numbers='one two three four five six',  /* (continuation) */
  'seven eight nine ten eleven twelve'
out=out word(numbers,hour)            /* add the hour number */
if min=0 then out=out "o'clock"    /* and o'clock if exact */

say out'.'                           /* display the final result */
exit

/*--------------------------------------------------------------*/
/* Subroutine that describes the purpose of the program    */
/*--------------------------------------------------------------*/
Tell:
  say 'QT will display the current time in natural English.'
  say 'Call without arguments to display the time, or with'
  say '"?" to display this information.  A second argument'
  say '(in the format "HH:MM:SS") will test the program.'
  say 'British English idioms are used in this program.'
  say     /* space - we are about to continue and show time */
  return

/* Mike Cowlishaw,  December 1979 - September 1989          */
```

Appendix C: Language Changes since First Edition

This appendix summarizes the changes in the REXX language in this edition (language version 4.00) compared to that defined in the first edition of this book (version 3.60).

The majority of changes are simply clarifications or improvements to the wording of the language definition (such as the more rigorous use of technical terms) which were generally made in response to feedback from readers and language implementers. These clarifications are not detailed here, though a glossary has been added (see page 179).

The remaining changes, listed here by relevant page number, are significant enhancements and improvements to the language or clarifications of description that could have been misinterpreted.

18   An implementation minimum for comments (nesting of at least 10 allowed) has been added.

20   Binary-defined literal strings have been added (for example, '1110 0111'b).

21   Characters defined as ambiguous in the ISO standard 7-bit encoding (*ISO 646 – Information processing – ISO 7-bit coded character set for information interchange*) have been removed from the set of characters valid for symbols to aid portability of REXX programs. The characters affected are the currency symbols (pound, dollar, and cent) and the hash

("pound", number) sign. The "at" sign has also been removed as this character is often ambiguous in national encodings.

43   ON and OFF have a special meaning for the CALL instruction (as noted on page 40 of the first edition) which has now been defined. CALL ON and CALL OFF are used to provide enhanced error handling (similar to SIGNAL ON and SIGNAL OFF, but with the possibility of return from the error routine).

45   Additional information (called *condition information*) is saved across a subroutine call.

47   TO, BY, and FOR are no longer reserved names within the WHILE or UNTIL phrases of the DO instruction. (This was an unnecessary restriction.)

49   The format of the initial value of a DO loop control variable is explicitly described.

53   DROP can now indirectly specify variables to be dropped (see also the PROCEDURE instruction, on page 65).

65   The EXPOSE list on a PROCEDURE instruction may indirectly include a list of variable names (using a syntax consistent with that of parsing templates). This makes it easier to share a list of variables to be exposed among several subroutines, and also permits a routine to deal with exposed variables whose names vary or are not known at the time of programming.

72   SIGNAL ON and SIGNAL OFF may specify the name of a label to which control will be passed if the condition occurs. This permits multiple handlers for the same condition in one REXX program; the name of the routine is no longer fixed. (The same flexibility is also allowed for CALL ON and CALL OFF.)

74   TRACE SCAN has been removed because it can be very expensive to implement and its function is better provided directly by modern smart editing systems, *etc.*

81   The treatment of numbers by "mathematical" functions was not always precisely described. It is now defined that numbers are reduced to standard format before use by these built-in functions.

83   The number of argument strings passed to a routine is now defined precisely.

85   B2X (binary to hexadecimal conversion) function has been added.

89   CONDITION function has been added. This is used for access to additional information about conditions that have been trapped: the name, description, and state of the condition, and the kind of trap (CALL or SIGNAL) are made available.

92   The Base option has been added to the DATE function. This returns a count of days since a theoretical base date of 1 January 0001.

The Century option for the DATE function has been removed because it is made obsolete by the Base option and its use is likely to lead to program errors at the start of a century.

105 The definition of the SOURCELINE function has been relaxed to permit flexibility in situations where the source of a REXX program is unavailable.

105 The STREAM function has been added. This function is used for querying the state of a stream or for carrying out system-dependent operations (commands) defined for a stream.

108 The elapsed time counter (used via the TIME function) implementation minimum has been relaxed to allow for operating systems with only coarse timing facilities.

112 The VALUE function has been enhanced to allow the setting of variables (hence avoiding many uses of INTERPRET). It can also now be used to retrieve or set variables selected from "pools" external to the language processor.

115 X2B (hexadecimal to binary conversion) function has been added.

123 An absolute column number in a parsing template can be indicated explicitly by an equals sign.

125 Variable references in parsing templates can now be used as column (positional) patterns by preceding the left parenthesis by an equals, plus, or minus sign.

130 The algorithm to be used for addition and subtraction has been clarified.

133 The power operator specifies a higher precision for the intermediate operations in the algorithm, in order to guarantee a comparable accuracy to the other arithmetic operations.

133 The Integer Division and Remainder operators are defined to fail (as an error) if the result of integer division cannot be expressed as a whole number. This prevents misleading or erroneous results being propagated through a calculation.

137 The description of whole numbers, and their use, has been consolidated and clarified.

138 The description of an overflow/underflow error has been made more rigorous.

142 Error handling during input and output has been enhanced by the addition of the NOTREADY condition. This state can be detected by condition trapping or by using the STREAM function.

145 The new section on conditions and condition traps consolidates the CALL ON and SIGNAL ON instructions and includes a number of clarifications and enhancements to the language.

160 Error 15 has been extended to allow for errors in binary strings.

161 Error 23 has been added to allow for character sets in which some encodings are invalid.

164 Error 46 has been added to allow better reporting of a common error in parsing templates.

Appendix D: Glossary

This glossary describes but does not define the technical terms used in the definition of the REXX language.

absolute positional pattern: A *positional pattern* that has no sign or has an equals sign; this specifies an absolute column position.

abuttal operator: When two terms in an expression are adjacent and are not separated by an operator, they are said to abut. Abutting two terms in this way implies the *abuttal operator* which has the same effect as the | | operator, that is, it concatenates the two terms (without a blank).

address setting: The currently selected *environment name*.

arguments: The expressions (separated by commas) between the parentheses on a function call or following the name on a CALL instruction. The arguments to a program, function, or subroutine can be retrieved by using the ARG or PARSE ARG instructions, or the ARG built-in function.

arithmetic operator: Character strings that are numbers (see page 27) may be combined using the arithmetic operators: add, subtract, multiply, divide, integer divide, remainder, power, prefix minus, and prefix plus.

ASCII: American Standard Code for Information Interchange; a set of *coded representations* for a specific set of *characters*.

assignment: A *clause* with the form *symbol = expression* is an instruction known as an assignment. An assignment gives a variable a (new) value.

binary string: A *literal string*, expressed using a binary representation of its encoding. The binary representation is a sequence of zero or more binary digits (the characters 0 or 1), grouped in fours.

blank operator: A *concatenation operator* that concatenates two strings with a blank in between, and which is represented by a blank.

built-in function: A *function* (which may be called as a *subroutine*) that is defined as part of the REXX language (see pages 81–117).

character: A member of a defined set of elements that is used for the control or representation of data. Often entered with a single keystroke.

character input stream: A character input stream is a serial character stream conceptually generated by user interaction, or having the characteristics of a stream generated in that manner, from which characters and/or lines may be read. See *stream*.

character output stream: A character output stream is a serial character stream to which characters and/or lines may be written. See *stream*.

character string: See *string*.

clause: The fundamental grouping of REXX syntax. Clauses are composed of: zero or more blanks (which are ignored); a sequence of tokens; zero or more blanks (again ignored); and the delimiter ";" (semicolon) which may be implied by line-end, certain keywords, or the colon ":" (if it follows a single symbol).

coded representation: The representation of a character established by a set of unambiguous rules specifying the manner in which the character can be represented in a discrete (digital) form.

command: A *clause* consisting of just an expression is an instruction known as a command. The expression is evaluated and the result is passed as a command string to some external environment.

comment: A piece of commentary that is started by the sequence of characters "/∗", and is ended by "∗/". Within these delimiters any characters are allowed. Comments may be nested.

comparative operator: An operator that compares two terms and returns the value 1 if the result of the particular comparison is true, or 0 otherwise.

compound symbol: A *symbol* that allows for the substitution of variables within its name, when referred to. It contains at least one period, and at least two other characters. It may not start with a digit or a period, and if there is only one period it may not be the last character. The name begins with a *stem* (that part of the symbol up to and including the first period). This is followed by the *tail* – parts of the name (delimited by periods) that are constant symbols, simple symbols, or null. Compound symbols allow the construction of arrays, associative tables, lists, *etc*.

concatenation operator: An operator used to combine two strings to form one string by appending the second string to the right-hand end of the first string. The concatenation may occur with or without an intervening blank.

condition: A specific event, or state, which can be trapped by CALL ON or SIGNAL ON. See page 145.

condition information: Information describing the state and origin of the *current trapped condition*. This information may be inspected by using the built-in function CONDITION (see page 89).

condition trap: The flow of execution in a REXX program is normally explicitly determined by the instructions in the program. Under certain conditions, however, the explicit flow may be modified by a *condition trap*. Condition traps are enabled or disabled using the ON or OFF sub-keywords of the CALL and SIGNAL instructions, and can be used to trap a variety of conditions, such as errors in commands, input, or output.

conditional phrase: A phrase in a DO instruction, introduced by the sub-keyword WHILE or UNTIL, that is used to modify the iteration of a *repetitive DO loop*.

constant symbol: A symbol that starts with a digit (0-9) or a period. The value of a constant symbol cannot be changed, and is simply the string consisting of the characters of the symbol with any alphabetic characters translated to upper case.

continuation character: If the last token on a line is a comma, it has the effect of disabling the implied semicolon normally added at the end of a line, and hence allows a clause to be continued across lines. The continuation character is replaced by a blank, and may be followed by one or more comments before the end of the line.

controlled repetitive loop: A *repetitive do loop* in which the repetitor phrase specifies a control variable. This variable is given an initial value before the first execution of the instruction list and is then stepped (by adding the result of an optional expression) before the second and subsequent times that the instruction list is executed.

current trapped condition: The most recently trapped *condition*.

delayed state: The state of a *condition trap* when the condition has been raised but the trap has not yet been reset to the enabled (ON) or disabled (OFF) state.

derived name: The default value of a compound symbol. This is the stem of the symbol, in uppercase, followed by the tail in which all simple symbols have been replaced by their value.

do group: The simplest form of DO instruction, in which no repetitor phrase or conditional phrase is specified. This construct groups a number of instructions together: these are executed once.

do loop: See *repetitive do loop.*

dyadic operator: An *operator* that acts on two terms.

EBCDIC: Extended Binary Coded Decimal Interchange Code; a set of *coded representations* for a specific set of *characters.*

encoding: A *coded representation.*

engineering notation: An *exponential notation* in which from one to three digits (but not just "0") will appear before the decimal point, and in which the power of ten will always be a multiple of three. Engineering notation can be selected using the NUMERIC FORM instruction. See also *scientific notation.*

environment name: The name of an external procedure or process that can execute *commands.* Commands are sent to the current environment, initially selected externally but then alterable by using the ADDRESS instruction.

error: A *condition* raised by a command for which a program that uses that command would normally be expected to be prepared. (For example, a Locate command to an editing system might report "requested string not found" as an error.) See also *failure.*

error number: The number, defined by the REXX language, assigned to errors that might be detected during processing of a REXX program. A description of the error can be retrieved using the ERRORTEXT built-in function.

exponential notation: A notation for expressing a number that includes an exponent (a power of ten by which the number is multiplied before use). See also *engineering notation, scientific notation.*

exposed variable: A variable belonging to an ancestor (caller) of a routine that has been made accessible by the PROCEDURE instruction. When referred to or altered by the routine, it is the original (ancestor's) copy of the variable that is used or affected.

expression: An expression in REXX is a general mechanism for combining one or more pieces of data in various ways to produce a result, usually different from the original data. Expressions include a mixture of *terms* and *operators.*

external data queue: A queue of character strings that is external to REXX programs in that other programs may have access to the queue whenever REXX relinquishes control to some other program. It can only be accessed by line operations.

external routine: A *function* or *subroutine* that is neither a *built-in routine* nor is in the same program as the CALL instruction or function call that invokes it.

failure: A *condition* raised by a command for which a program that uses that command would **not** normally be expected to recover (for example, if the command was not executable or could not be found). See also *error*.

function: An internal, built-in, or external routine that returns a single result string and is invoked by a *function call*. A function can also be invoked by the CALL instruction, in which case it is being called as a *subroutine*.

function call: A *term* in an expression which invokes a routine that carries out some procedure and then returns a string. This string then replaces the function call for the continuing evaluation of the expression. A function call is identified by a symbol that is immediately followed by a left parenthesis.

fuzz: The amount by which two numbers may differ before being considered equal for the purpose of comparison. The fuzz value is set by the NUMERIC FUZZ instruction; its effect is to temporarily reduce the value of NUMERIC DIGITS by the NUMERIC FUZZ value for each numeric comparison. See page 135.

guard digit: An extra digit used during arithmetic operations to improve the accuracy of the computation. The guard digit is inspected at the end of the operation when the number is rounded to the required *precision*.

hexadecimal string: A *literal string*, expressed using a hexadecimal representation of its encoding. The hexadecimal representation is a sequence of zero or more hexadecimal digits (the characters 0-9, a-f, A-F) grouped in pairs.

implied semicolon: REXX will normally assume (imply) a semicolon at the end of each line, except if the line ends in the middle of a comment or the last token was a *continuation character* (comma).

instruction: One or more *clauses* that describe some course of action to be taken by the language processor. Instructions may be either Assignments, Keyword Instructions, or Commands.

interactive trace: A form of *trace* during which the programmer is given the opportunity of interacting with the language processor as the program is executed.

internal routine: A *function* or *subroutine* that is in the same program as the CALL instruction or function call that invokes it.

keyword instruction: One or more *clauses*, the first of which starts with a keyword that identifies the instruction. Keyword instructions control the external interfaces, the flow of control, and so on. Some keyword instructions (such as DO) can include nested instructions.

label: A *clause* that consists of a single symbol followed by a colon. The colon in this context implies a semicolon (clause separator), and so a label is a clause in its own right and no semicolon is required. Labels are used to identify the targets of CALL instructions, SIGNAL instructions, and internal function calls; more than one label may precede any instruction. Labels are treated as null clauses, and may be traced selectively to aid debugging.

literal pattern: See *pattern*.

literal string: A sequence including **any** characters and delimited by the single quote character (') or the double-quote ("). Literal strings are constant (cannot be modified) and are used to express data within a REXX program.

monadic operator: See *prefix operator*.

name: A symbol that names some component of the REXX language, such as a variable or a function.

normal comparison: An operation that compares two strings in different ways depending on their content: if both strings are numbers then a numeric comparison is used, otherwise a character comparison (in which leading and trailing blanks are ignored) is effected. See also *strict comparison*.

null clause: A *clause* consisting of only blanks and/or comments. Null clauses are ignored by REXX, except for tracing.

null string: A *string* with no characters (that is, a string of length 0).

number: A character string consisting of one or more decimal digits optionally prefixed by a plus or minus sign, and optionally including a single period (".") which then represents a decimal point. A number may also have a power of ten suffixed in conventional exponential notation: an "E" (upper or lower case) followed optionally by a plus or minus sign then followed by one or more decimal digits defining the power of ten. Numbers may have leading blanks (before and/or after the sign, if any) and may have trailing blanks. Blanks may not be embedded among the digits of a number or in the exponential part.

operator: A representation of an operation, such as addition, that is to be carried out on one or two *terms*. Operators are specified using various combinations of *operator characters*.

operator character: One of the characters + - * / % | & = ¬ \ > < which are used (sometimes in combination) to indicate operators in expressions (see pages 25–27).

pad character: A character used to extend a string, usually on the right. See, for example, the LEFT built-in function (on page 98).

parse: To decompose a string into parts; in REXX this can be done by function calls or by using a parsing *template* on the ARG, PARSE, or PULL instructions.

pattern: The parts of a parsing *template* that allow a string to be split up by the explicit matching of strings (*literal patterns*) or by the specification of numeric positions (*positional patterns*). Parentheses may be supplied to create a *variable pattern* – a pattern whose value is derived from a variable.

placeholder: The symbol consisting of a single period acts as a placeholder in a parsing *template*. It has exactly the same effect as a variable name, except that no variable is set.

positional pattern: See *pattern*.

precision: The maximum number of significant digits that can result from an arithmetic operation. This is controlled by the NUMERIC DIGITS instruction; the default is 9 digits.

prefix (monadic) operator: An *operator* that acts on a single term, which is immediately to the right of the operator. There may be one or more prefix operators to the left of any term.

read position: The position in a *character input stream* from which the next character or line will be read.

recursive routine: A subroutine or function that calls or invokes itself (possibly indirectly).

relative positional pattern: A *positional pattern* that uses a plus or minus sign to indicate movement relative to a previous pattern match.

repetitive do loop: Any DO instruction that has either a repetitor phrase or a conditional phrase (or both). The instruction list within the instruction is executed zero or more times, controlled by any repetitor phrase which is optionally modified by a conditional phrase.

repetitor phrase: A phrase in a DO instruction that is used to specify the iteration of a *repetitive DO loop*. This may be an expression that evaluates to a whole number, a control variable and its bounds, or the sub-keyword FOREVER.

return code: A string, typically a number passed in an implementation-dependent way, that conveys some information about the command that has been executed. Return codes usually indicate the success or failure of the command but can also be used to represent other information.

scientific notation: An *exponential notation* in which only one, non-zero, digit will appear before the decimal point. Scientific notation can be selected using the NUMERIC FORM instruction, and is the default. See also *engineering notation*.

simple do group: See *do group*.

simple repetitive loop: A *repetitive do loop* in which the repetitor phrase is simply an expression that evaluates to a count of iterations.

simple symbol: A symbol that does not contain any periods and does not start with a digit (0-9). By default its value is the characters of the symbol (translated to upper case). If the symbol has been assigned a value, it names a variable and its value is the value of that variable.

special character: The characters ,   ;   :   )   (together with the *operator characters* have special significance when found outside of literal strings, and constitute the set of "special" characters.

special variable: A variable that may be set automatically during execution of a REXX program. There are three: RC, RESULT, and SIGL. None of these has an initial value. They may be altered by the program, just like any other variable, but will continue to be set automatically by REXX when appropriate.

stem: That part of a *compound symbol* up to and including the first period. If used alone (so that the symbol itself contains just one period, which is the last character) the default value of a stem is the characters of its symbol, translated to upper case. A reference to a stem can also be used to manipulate all variables sharing that stem (PROCEDURE EXPOSE, DROP, and so on).

stream: The REXX language defines only simple, character oriented, forms of input and output. In general, communication to or from the user is in the form of a stream of characters. These *streams* may be manipulated either character-by-character or line-by-line. They may be a channel of communication with a human user, but in many environments the character streams manipulated might have a variety of sources or destinations, such as files, serial interfaces, displays, or networks. They may be transient (for example, data sent or received over a serial interface) or they may be persistent (for example, files and objects).

stream command: An implementation-defined stream operation, issued using the STREAM built-in function. The stream command mechanism is provided to allow for operating environments that have special requirements for the manipulation of certain input or output streams.

strict comparison: An operation that compares two strings on a strict character-by-character basis. Two strings must be identical for them to be considered strictly equal. See also *normal comparison*.

string: A linear (one-dimensional) series of *characters*.

sub-expression: A *term* in an expression that consists of any expression bracketed by a left and a right parenthesis.

sub-keyword: A keyword that is reserved within the context of some particular instruction – for example the symbols TO and WHILE in the DO instruction. For a general discussion on reserved words, see page 154.

subroutine: An internal, built-in, or external routine that may or may not return a result string and is invoked by the CALL instruction. If it returns a result string, a subroutine can also be invoked by a *function call*, in which case it is being called as a *function*.

symbol: A symbol is a group of any characters selected from the English alphabetic and numeric characters (A-Z, a-z, 0-9) and/or from the characters . ! ? and underscore. Symbols are used to name variables, functions, instructions, *etc.*

tail: The part of a *compound symbol* that follows the *stem*. It may include constant symbols, simple symbols, and periods.

template: Three instructions (ARG, PARSE, and PULL) allow a selected string to be parsed (split up) and assigned to variables, under the control of a *template*. The various mechanisms in the template allow a string to be split up by words (delimited by blanks), or by explicit matching of strings (called *literal patterns*), or by specifying numeric positions – for example to extract data from particular columns of a line read from a character stream (*positional patterns*).

term: A literal string, symbol, function call, or sub-expression, which represents a character string used within an expression. Terms are combined using *operators*.

token: The unit of low-level syntax from which *clauses* are built. Tokens include literal strings, symbols, operator characters, and special characters. See page 19.

trace: A description of some or all of the clauses in a program, produced as each is executed. Tracing is the simplest form of debugging aid.

typeless character string: A *string*. REXX strings are described as "typeless" because they are not (as in many other programming languages) of a particular, declared type, such as binary, hexadecimal, integer, or array.

uninitialized variable: A variable that has not yet been assigned a value. If referred to, its value is the character(s) of the symbol itself, translated to upper case (unless it is a compound symbol, in which case its value is the *derived name* of the symbol).

variable: A *variable* is a named object whose value may be changed during the course of execution of a REXX program. The process of changing the value of a variable is called *assigning* a new value to it. The value of a variable is a single character string, of any length, that may contain any characters.

variable pattern: See *pattern*.

variable reference: An indirect reference to a variable in which the value of the variable is used rather than its name. This is indicated by enclosing the name in parentheses, and can be used on the DROP and PROCEDURE instructions, and in parsing *templates*.

whole number: A *number* that has a zero (or no) decimal part, and which would not normally be expressed by REXX in exponential notation – that is, it has no more digits before the decimal point than the current setting of NUMERIC DIGITS (the default is nine digits).

word: A sequence of characters that does not include any blanks. Words are used as units for manipulation during parsing and by many built-in functions.

write position: The position in a *character output stream* at which the next character or line will be written.

Index